Developing Attachment in Early Years Settings

Developing Attachment in Early Years Settings is a guide for practitioners to help them prepare for the care of individual babies and children in their settings. This highly practical book offers the reader advice on implementing attachment principles in line with the Practice Guidance of the Early Years Foundation Stage and the Early Years National Strategy – Social and Emotional Aspects of Development (SEAD) 2008. Explaining the importance of emotional 'holding' and the nurturing of individual relationships within group childcare, this book will help readers develop an understanding of how to:

- facilitate secure attachments from the beginning
- create a secure base for key children
- observe young children effectively.

Each chapter includes a personal reflection exercise and a positive contribution to good practice section. With its accessible approach, this book is essential reading for both practitioners and students looking for guidance on how to nurture secondary attachment relationships in group care settings.

Veronica Read is a Group Analyst and an Independent Educational Consultant. She writes and delivers workshops on attachment for Early Years practitioners. She also works for an LEA as a Behaviour Support Teacher in a Specialist Teaching Team and has extensive experience of working with children with social, emotional and behavioural difficulties.

Developing Attachment in Early Years Settings

Nurturing secure relationships from birth to five years

Veronica Read

R Routledge
Taylor & Francis Group

LONDON AND NEW YORK

First published 2010
by Routledge
2 Park Square, Milton Park, Abingdon, Oxon OX14 4RN

Simultaneously published in the USA and Canada
by Routledge
270 Madison Ave, New York, NY 10016

Routledge is an imprint of the Taylor & Francis Group, an informa business

Typeset in Bembo and Frutiger by Book Now Ltd, London
Printed and bound in Great Britain by TJ International Ltd, Padstow,
Cornwall

British Library Cataloguing in Publication Data
A catalogue record for this book is available from the British Library

Library of Congress Cataloging in Publication Data
Read, Veronica.
Developing attachment in Early Years settings: nurturing secure
relationships from birth to five years / Veronica Read.
      p. cm.
Includes bibliographical references.
1. Child care services—Great Britain. 2. Attachment behavior in infants—
Great Britain. 3. Attachment behavior in children—Great Britain. I. Title.
HQ778.7.G7R43 2010
155.42′28—dc22   2009015765

ISBN10: 0–415–49163–0 (hbk)
ISBN10: 0–415–49164–9 (pbk)
ISBN10: 0–203–87105–7 (ebk)

ISBN13: 978–0–415–49163–1 (hbk)
ISBN13: 978–0–415–49164–8 (pbk)
ISBN13: 978–0–203–87105–8 (ebk)

For Hannah and John

Contents

Figures

Acknowledgements

I wish to acknowledge my first hearing of the Tavistock Clinic from my father who had visited it regularly when he worked in the area of Child Welfare for the London County Council in the 1950s. This was at a time when 'the Minister of Health issued a directive asking the London County Council to pay more attention to mental health' (Holmes 1993).

Although, he never referred directly to the influence of Bowlby, my father described being drawn to the child development thinking which flourished at the Tavistock and helped him in his challenging work in the White City area of London. Having experienced the death of his mother at a very early age, perhaps it was a place where he could gain some understanding into his own early distress as well as meeting the needs of the many children and families with whom he worked.

In many ways this book is all about how practitioners can manage their own responses and emotions in the face of young children's distress and through reflective practice continue to nurture and develop secure attachments.

I wish to thank Anita Hughes for suggesting I might have a contribution to make in the running of workshops for Early Years practitioners. With huge generosity she offered me a wonderful opportunity to share in delivering a training she had developed, which introduces key carers of 0–3 year olds to the importance of meaningful secondary attachments . She has been instrumental in encouraging me to plant the seed of this book and supported me with great kindness in bringing it to fruition.

I would like to express my deep appreciation to colleagues, family and friends over the years who have contributed to the foundations of this book and who have helped me think this book through in various ways long before its conception. They are Sarah Balingall, Michael Howlett, Sarah Lea,

Amanda Lett, Bev Selway, Vivien Norris, Tess Miller, Justin Read, Ewa Wojciechowska, Linda Evans, Carol Rowe, and Peter Wilson.

I owe so much to the experience I had as a wife and mother at Peper Harrow, Surrey where I was introduced to the thinking of Bettleheim, Winnicott and Bowlby by Michael Maher.

I am grateful for the teaching on Attachment Theory I received when training at the Institute of Group Analysis in London and in particular for the generous and inspiring communication of ideas by Mario Marrone and Felicity de Zulueta.

My thanks go to Dr Karl Heinz-Brisch for his energy and enthusiasm in his communication of Attachment Theory and the inspiring annual Attachment Conferences at the University of Munich, making the subject accessible to a wide multi-professional audience. This book began in Germany.

It has been very satisfying professionally to have the encouragement of Gerda Hanko, who has supported my development of collaborative problem-solving groups for staff working in Early Years settings.

Most recently, I wish to thank Dr Una McCluskey for her clarity of thought and facilitation of the Exploring the Dynamics of Attachment in Adult Life Group and for keeping myself and the other group members always in a state of curiosity, discovery and vitality.

I would also like to thank Michelle Dows-Miller, the children, staff and parents at the Weyhill Montessori, Haslemere. Thank you, too Anya and Finn.

I am indebted to Susan Birt-Price and Kirsty Stickley for offering me such wonderful teaching opportunities. I am grateful for the many work-shop participants who have warmly welcomed me across into their profes-sional world, deepened my understanding and shared their expertise so generously with me.

I am deeply grateful to my group during my training at the Institute of Group Analysis and especially to Dr Earl Hopper, PhD, my Training Analyst, for his commitment to helping me understand the hope inherent in mean-ingful attachments being a lifelong process.

Finally, thank you Hannah and John for being such an inspiration to me.

Foreword

I am so delighted that Veronica has at last written a book which lucidly explains what the principles of attachment behaviour mean in relation to group childcare and the key person approach. She has successfully described the importance of 'secondary attachments' in ways that speak directly to the people who look after babies and young children on a daily basis.

The reader is drawn into a narrative, where the stories and accounts are woven into a beautiful tapestry that take one on a journey of understanding how important early relationships between infants and carers are in a very real rather than theoretical way. She has managed to translate the principles of Attachment Theory into a framework for thinking that is both relevant and easy to understand.

What I particularly like is the blend of the personal accounts alongside practical guidance for practitioners. Veronica has referred to the EYFS in a clear manner, but the content of this book will outlive government legislation and have relevance to practitioners for many years to come. This is because Veronica has vividly described the emotional experience of being a carer. She has also clearly illustrated and explained both the challenges and hopes of meaningful secondary attachments, which underpin group childcare, whether it is in a nursery or in a private home. As the percentage of very young children experiencing care outside the family home increases, the need to understand the vital importance of secure secondary attachments becomes ever more pressing in our society.

What is also unusual about this book and is a refreshing aspect is that it seeks to invite the reader to ask questions and reflect upon their own practice. Many books written for Early Years Practitioners simply tell the reader what they should do to improve their practice. Whilst there is place for such books, understanding how we might create loving relationships with babies and young children is more about the emotional experience than about the intellectual exercise. This book satisfies the intellect whilst bravely exploring the deep emotional experience working with young children gives. It is also written in a lucid and pleasing style which will be accessible to all those working in the field of the early years.

In many ways, the seeds of this book were sown about 15 years ago, when Veronica and I were working together, running groups for adolescent girls in a challenging urban comprehensive school. These girls had serious behavioural problems and were regularly being excluded from school. Their families were disrupted and unsettled and so were they. However, through the experience of having a 'secure base' through the group, these girls began to develop more secure attachments and gain in confidence. They also became more responsible and caring towards others and were happier and more positive about life. It gave Veronica and I our first real taste of the potency of facilitating meaningful secondary attachments and how they can have a direct impact on the quality of life.

The importance that practitioners make in the lives of babies and young children cannot be underestimated. This book recognises and embraces this and will give those who read it a sense of hope for the future.

Anita M. Hughes
April 2009

Introduction

When you drive through any village, town or city in the United Kingdom today, you will notice a significant change in the landscape. Every few miles travelled will reveal a succession of bold, decorative boards bearing such names as Little Acorns, Caring Daycare, Poppets, Sticky Mits, Kiddiwinks, Children's Centre and so on. These familiar signs map the expansion of group day care over the last decade in every locality, offering care for babies, infants and pre-school children. The message is clear as we drive by: there is an important shift in the way children are being brought up in this country.

Rarely do I pass a roadside nursery these days without looking at the surrounding space each building looks out over and I scan for the signs of the natural world, hoping that children will have outdoor space that allows them to see a changing world and the green shoots of nature in the springtime. My mind also goes to the interior of these places and I think of the image of a nursing mother and infant and wonder whether practitioners are 'making do' and propping themselves up against radiators as they feed the babies in their care. This text is about the importance of quiet, rhythmical times with young children and finding space, supported by a well-upholstered, comfy chair to feed infants with love and care. If we 'make do' and do not receive and give ourselves as practitioners the support we require as caregivers then our ability to offer authentic love and care to those who seek care will be diminished.

The aim of the Early Years Foundation Stage (EYFS) framework is to help young children achieve the five Every Child Matters outcomes by offering daily opportunities for the best possible start in life and encouraging effective practice aimed at supporting the five outcomes:

1. staying safe
2. being healthy
3. enjoying and achieving
4. making a positive contribution
5. achieving economic well-being.

Personal, social and emotional development is the bedrock upon which the (EYFS) framework is built as well as being one of the six areas covered by early learning goals. The aim of this book is to support practitioners and students in the area that focuses on personal, social and emotional development at the same time as emphasising it is also the background against which *all* six early learning goals feature. The six areas are:

1. personal, social and emotional development
2. communication, language and literacy
3. problem-solving, reasoning and numeracy
4. knowledge and understanding of the world
5. physical development
6. creative development.

This book aims to help practitioners think and reflect on the small but significant steps they can take to really identify with children and their needs, and from that place build genuine attachments and view vulnerability as an opportunity to strengthen both the careseeker and caregiver. This book will help practitioners:

*   nurture warm secondary attachments;
*   understand the verbal and non-verbal communications children offer you;
*   notice what you are feeling as you observe children;
*   quietly and confidently meet the changing needs of children;
*   develop by your reflective presence, resilience in young children.

Chapters 3, 4, 5 and 6 relate to the four commitments of the EYFS:

1. unique child
2. positive relationships

3. enabling environment
4. learning and development.

Practitioners through their commitment to the practice guidance are being encouraged to provide settings where children are:

- perceived as special/well cared for;
- experiencing a sense of belonging;
- free to express their feelings;
- developing coping strategies;
- developing positive ideas about themselves and others;
- acknowledged and affirmed.

The book will show how facilitating secure attachments is central to meeting the requirements of the EYFS framework, which has at its heart the importance of all children being special and attached, leading to a secure place in society and authentic citizenship for all throughout their lives.

We now know due to advances and research on brain development that the key building blocks for emotional well-being, good mental health and future success in life are developed through close, loving and intimate relationships. The Early Years National Strategy – Social and Emotional Aspects of Development (SEAD) 2008 emphasises the importance of being knowledgeable about child development and developing empathic skills in young children. Secondary caregivers are giving meaning to an infant and young child's feelings by supporting them in the process of discovering about:

- being me
- being social
- having feelings.

This core development of a child's inner world is how we all come to:

- understand ourselves in relation to others;
- make friends;
- behave towards others;
- later understand society's rules.

There is an underlying expectation that practitioners will be reflective in their practice and look, listen and note in detail, the social and emotional aspects of the learning processes they observe. By listening seriously to what is said and done, and putting their insights to good use, the path is laid down to meet learning goals. Through the establishment of a culture of respect that believes in parents as the first and most enduring educators, professionals and parents can work together and have a positive impact on children's development and learning.

This book is also about leading rather than managing the vision and ethos of the EYFS.

Leading the EYFS agenda in any setting requires creating an organisational setting which reflects the secure attachment skills of managers. Managers have an important role in working with the whole staff team and celebrating:

- the unique individuals in the room;
- the positive relationships between staff;
- the enabling environment of the EYFS framework;
- the continuing professional development and learning of all practitioners.

As I complete the writing of this book, and in the wake of the introduction of the Early Years Foundation Stage (EYFS) in September 2008, The Innocenti Report Card 8: The Childcare Transition (Adamson 2008) has been published by UNICEF. This report looks at the growth of Early Years childcare and notes:

> Across the industrialized nations, out-of-home child care is a fact of life for ever more children at ever earlier ages and for ever longer hours.

It highlights the fact that in the United Kingdom for example, a majority of mothers are now returning to full or part-time work within 12 months of giving birth.

At the same time as this flourishing of Early Years provision, we are also becoming aware of the advances in research on brain development and the importance of careseeking and caregiving relationships as the secure foundation for healthy emotional and intellectual development. Equally, sensitive 'tuning in' to a child's emotional state – their internal world – helps in the development of empathy.

This book is about encouraging the wisdom of individual practitioners and teams of staff committed to enhancing the early life chances of infants and young children. At the heart of this process is the importance of believing that high quality services that meet the needs of the disadvantaged and those with special and additional needs can become a template for good practice for all children. Having the capacity to care and to attune to individual children has now become the responsibility of caregiving settings beyond the family.

We need however to be mindful that for babies and children under three who enter a group childcare setting there is a potentially stressful set of challenges to be met by them. How these anxieties are received and reflected upon depends upon the quality of training practitioners receive, as well as how we in society reward and respect them for the important role they are being asked to take on.

Each chapter in the book includes a practitioner's account, how to make a positive contribution to good practice, a section for your personal reflections and links to the EYFS and the National Strategy – Social and Emotional Aspects of Development (SEAD). It is hoped that practitioners will be able to see clearly through the reading of this book how healthy attachment is the golden thread that runs through the rich and colourful tapestry of the Early Years Foundation Stage.

The case studies described in the book are based on recurring themes accumulated over a number of years. They represent an amalgam of material and any identifying details have been removed to preserve confidentiality.

Beginnings

A practitioner's account

Khalid aged 15 months is waiting at the gate.

Fifteen-month-old Khalid has been going to nursery two afternoons a week for a few weeks now. He clings and cries as his mother leaves. Once she has left, he wanders around the room unable to settle and often stands at the gated doorway looking out. He does not join in with the other children in his group. One of his carers, Sally, says that he seems unable to settle to play and that he is not attached to her or the other staff. She has begun to feel overwhelmed by this situation as she is uncertain about what to do. The only time Khalid appears more settled is when he is sitting securely in his high chair having his afternoon snack. His mother has shared with Sally the fact that he is still being breastfed at home where he has begun communicating happily with other members of his bilingual family. Sally has also discovered during a tearful conversation with Khalid's mother that she fled Iraq seven years ago. She has expressed a wish too that Khalid does not leave the play area for the afternoon walk to the local duck pond, which the other children take regularly with staff. So, each afternoon, he stands at the nursery gate watching them set off. Khalid does not have a key person as he is not at nursery full-time.

I have begun this book with an account of a child's experience of nursery as seen through the eyes of one of his carers, because I expect you have known a child like Khalid. Perhaps you have a child currently in your care who cannot tell you how they are feeling. Yet like Sally, you sense their unsettledness and because you care, this matters to you.

We can never remind ourselves too often that a child particularly a very young and almost dependent one, is the only person in the nursery who cannot understand why he is there.

(Goldschmied and Jackson 1994: 42)

Attachment and separation

Attachment Theory is a way of explaining the emotional bonds that children develop with their carers, how crucial these are to their personal, social and emotional development and what we observe when a child is separated from the secure relationship of their primary caregiver. This important first relationship and the enabling environment of his extended family is what has sustained Khalid since birth. With many more children entering group day care younger, this first experience of separation is happening much earlier for young children at a time when they are unable to understand fully what is happening.

What does Khalid need? He needs someone older, wiser and willing to make a close and special relationship with him to manage the loss he is feeling.

We will come back to Khalid throughout the book and meet other children, too. For it is through nurturing secure attachment relationships with such children that safe and enjoyable exploration of the world can begin for them.

As a practitioner wishing to understand the processes of attachment and separation, it is important to be able to see amid the free flow of activity in your settings the children, like Khalid, who are standing at the gate uncertain about how to take the next step forward or even to step back to a place of safety before moving forward again. This delicate transition requires time and practitioners can best respond to children by:

- allowing time and space to observe;
- listening with care;
- responding accurately;
- attending appropriately to babies, toddlers and reception class children;
- acknowledging that at points of change children can regress before taking the next step forward.

This is a book about being there for all those children waiting at the gate like Khalid, who seek care as they cross back and forth each day between their primary caregivers (parents) and their secondary caregivers (practitioners). How caregivers respond at these moments of change for children is the key to their future well-being. Children need to trust other significant adults and so have their needs understood and met. Is it significant that Khalid's mother has had to deal with a traumatic separation from her homeland a number of years ago as she separates from her son?

If you are interested in:

- understanding what young children are experiencing;
- understanding how children develop within the context of a secure attachment relationship;
- actively repairing and offering continuing relationships with toddlers as they explore their independence;
- developing a genuine curiosity like Sally;
- listening carefully to yourself when *you* feel overwhelmed;
- discovering what you feel when a child is distressed and how such feelings may be very important information about what a child is feeling;
- trusting that children may be asking you to hold a feeling for them, which they cannot manage temporarily;
- reflecting upon your practice;
- allowing yourself to begin to offer comfort and nurture naturally when children are separated from their primary caregivers;

… then let us begin.

Childhood

Once upon a time, childhood did not exist as we know it and Khalid's quiet distress may have gone unnoticed. It might be hard for us to imagine a world where a child's personal, social and emotional needs were not considered as important. Can you imagine a time when the health and education of children was not a regular talking point with the adults caring for them? Thankfully, finding time to notice and share our observations about children with colleagues is now an important and valued part of Early Years practice.

For many centuries, however, due to high rates of maternal and infant death, finding time to think about a child's developmental needs might have been a luxury. Perhaps, parents were unable to imagine their children's futures, due to them mourning the deaths of previous babies as a result of incurable childhood illnesses. Many of you will remember too, from your history lessons, that children up until the late nineteenth century entered the adult world of dirty and dangerous work, as young as seven years old and so did not enjoy a childhood as we now know it in the developed world.

There have also been times of national emergency, like during the Second World War when children needed to be sent to places of safety in a hurry. Groups of evacuated children with labels attached to their coats, carrying their gas masks were put on to trains and sent to the safety of the country. Society believed this was the best way to care for a child's physical safety. As adults, many of these evacuees have been able to tell us about how such experiences of separation did not make them feel emotionally safe and we have learned important lessons from their stories.

The Early Years Foundation Stage (EYFS)

The most recent changes that have taken place over the last 10 years in terms of care of young children have been the numbers of children (500,000) being looked after in Early Years group day care. In recent years, and most recently in September 2008, with the Early Years Foundation Stage (EYFS) there have been a number of curriculum changes, meaning staff, parents and children have had to get used to a great deal of change. As children are presented with lots of new experiences at a much earlier age, Early Years practitioners will know that although changes may come and go, children do not change and the joy for them is about meeting their needs so they grow and flourish.

Identifying with young children

It would require a whole new book to tell the story of how relationships between children and adults have changed over centuries and recent years, so for the purposes of this book, I will simply say that we have learned now that childhood really matters and that it is worth thinking about.

However, it is not easy thinking about a baby or identifying with a baby, perhaps because of the very fact that they cannot talk to us about what they are feeling. Attunement according to Stern (1985) is when the mother is on the same wavelength as the baby, her response matching closely the feeling (affect) state of the baby in terms of the vitality of continually changing

Figure 1.1 Developing a capacity to be curious, explore and think in the presence of a reassuring adult

emotional states. She does not imitate the baby's behaviour but helps match the intensity of experience and so helps regulate intense affect states. This reciprocal communication requires empathy from the adult and lays down the early traces of empathy in the baby.

Therefore, as a practitioner, a good place to start feeling alongside babies, young children and their parents is to:

- be aware of one's own experiences of childhood;
- share generously one's knowledge of child development with peers and parents;
- remain curious and reflective.

Understanding childhood from an attachment perspective

How does attachment research help us understand early childhood? There are many different ways of thinking about childhood. Attachment research focuses on the importance of good enough early relationships, as one of the most important building blocks for good emotional well-being and mental health in later life. When I use the term attachment I mean the unique relationship between a child and his primary caregiver that consists of numerous moment to moment interactions which fosters future healthy development. It is important that secondary attachment caregivers develop close and lasting relationships with the absent primary caregiver in order to successfully meet a child's needs during that absence. Bowlby defines attachment behaviour as 'any form of behaviour that results in a person attaining or maintaining proximity to some other clearly defined individual who is conceived as better able to cope with the world' (Bowlby 1988).

Many of our early experiences may be beyond our control, for example:

- our genetic inheritance;
- the environment of the womb;
- when and where we were born;
- the social, economic and cultural circumstances of the family we are born into.

However our genes shape our future, we are all from the moment of birth dependent upon others for our survival and so 'a gene cannot express itself, or have an influence, without its intimate partner – the environment' (Brazelton and Greenspan 2000). We know now too that this very early social environment shapes our emotional development and lays down a model for future relationships. The quality of preparation that goes into the fostering of long-term secondary caregiving and the commitment to authentic shared nurturing is within the control of a society committed to the protection of children.

Making relationships outside the family

Staff working in group childcare, give a great deal of imaginative thought to the environments they create, by making them warm, inviting, exciting and interesting places to welcome children into. If you become really curious about how each child sees and experiences this world around them, then that will include being interested in how children relate to and experience *you* as a person and secondary attachment figure. As practitioners you create the emotional climate and environment around the children in your care. After all, children's worlds extend not only to new places and things much earlier now but also to making important relationships with new people outside their family group at an earlier age.

Many of you may remember your first big step into the outside world being at about five years old, when you had a new experience called 'going to school'. There may have been lots of talking and preparation for this special day. You may not only remember the name of your first teacher but you may have a memory of something very specific and unique about that person. What would it be that would stick in your mind I wonder, about those first days at school?

With the expansion of Early Years group childcare, we are asking children to take greater emotional journeys earlier. Let us look at some of the challenges for young children setting off on such emotional journeys.

The challenges for babies

- Being held, fed and changed by someone unfamiliar.
- Reaching out for an unfamiliar finger, item of clothing, strand of hair or button on a blouse while feeding.
- The loss of a familiar person for several hours a week and the taking in of a new person.
- Adjusting to the pitch of a different voice.
- The smell of a new person.
- Listening to the rhythm of a heart beat as they rest against the chest of a new carer – is one heart beat really much like another, I wonder?
- Hearing unfamiliar sounds like the whirring of the air conditioning in the baby room or lots of other babies in close proximity crying at regular intervals.

The challenges for toddlers

- Entering a new and unfamiliar space.
- Being in a room full of new faces.
- Walking away from a primary caregiver for the first time.
- Realising that their special person up until this point is out of sight for an uncertain amount of time.
- Walking towards a new set of arms for safety.

- Learning to trust these new people to take care of them.

- Setting off on new adventures without being held in the gaze of a primary carer.

- Feeling safe enough to maintain new exploration on a daily basis.

Early years practitioners are like mountain sherpas

Early years practitioners accompany infants and young children as they take in a set of new experiences during the first moments, hours, days and months in their new setting. In so doing you share many of the qualities of Tibetan mountain sherpas (men) or sherpini (women), who accompany mountaineers on their climbs to new places:

- They were of immeasurable value to early explorers due to their offers of support.

- They are well suited to the climb due to their expertise and knowledge of the landscape.

- They have a quiet, hopeful and generous outlook in the face of difficulty.

It is important to value the building of an emotional base camp for children, by being in relationship with them. It will enable them to feel supported in their exploration, curiosity and learning. John Bowlby, the father of attachment thinking, called this a secure base, a trusted figure from whom to set off and to return to as a safe haven, whenever necessary. Being in relationship with a trusted and responsive adult allows a child to return to base, to emotionally refuel and recover before setting off again, curious and hopeful that the next new experience can be managed.

John Bowlby (1907–87), the father of Attachment Theory

John Bowlby, the father of Attachment Theory, first drew our attention to the ways in which adults and children:

- communicate and develop in relation to each other in the first years of life;

- respond when they are presented with real-life events which make them feel anxious and frightened.

Who was John Bowlby?

- He was born in 1907.

- He was the fourth of six children.

- His parents were middle aged by the time he was born.

- Parents at this time were often more distant in their parenting than they might be today.

- His primary carers were his nurse maid, Minnie and his nanny, Nanny Friend.

- His parents like many others at this time *may* have been preoccupied by talk of war.

- During the First World War (1914–18) his father was dealing directly with loss as an army surgeon.

- In 1914, aged 7 John was sent to boarding school with his brother.

- John was a successful student.

- After a brief period in the Navy, he chose a career in medicine, like his father.

- When he left Cambridge he decided to work with disturbed adolescents.

- He became interested in the link between children's early lives and their later disturbance.

- He developed an interest in psychoanalysis and child psychiatry.

- His thinking about early parent–child relationships developed against the background of the Second World War (1939–45).

- His new thinking about child development and the importance of a child's early environment occurred at the same time as the bombed environment of London was being rebuilt and many were coming to terms with their losses as a result of the war.

Why have I listed some key biographical details of Bowlby's life?

- To illustrate to the reader how we are the sum of many events and experiences, even before we are born.

- To show, as with John Bowlby, that the age into which we are born and all that goes on around us has an influence on the person we will become.

- To remind ourselves that every child who enters a nursery or children's centre is the sum of a whole range of unique experiences, too.

- As a reminder that each child has a story so far and to respect this fact each time we greet a new baby or child and so become genuinely curious about children before they even arrive into our care.

Just as when a modern, new building goes up alongside an old piece of architecture, it often becomes a talking point, so Bowlby's Attachment Theory met with a lot of hostility from his colleagues.

What was Bowlby saying that was different?

- He differed from the most influential figures in the field of psychoanalysis at the Tavistock Clinic, London by considering how the early environment influenced a developing child.

- He believed that real-life events were very important in a child's development.

- His studies revealed the effects of the loss of a primary caregiver and of there being no secure base for children.

- He observed that unexpected and prolonged separation in children revealed a reaction similar to grief.

- He identified a grieving process in the young that followed a pattern: protest, despair, detachment.

Being curious as a practitioner

How can we best prepare ourselves with this knowledge to accompany infants and young children on their journeys? How can we understand what happens to the world inside a child as they set out on a journey into new experiences? 'Although the attachment system and the exploratory system originate in opposing motivations, they exist in a state of interdependence' (Brisch 2002). Children are able to explore their environment with confidence if they know in the background there is a responsive and emotionally available adult.

Sensitive observation guides us to notice and respond to the messages given out by children as they meet new experiences. They guide us by the way they stand, their facial expressions, verbal and non-verbal communications and in so doing, invite us to respond to those cues. If we meet young children's needs and respond to their cues appropriately and promptly, then worry and anxiety lessens and inner security grows. Children are, therefore, better able to hope that difficult feelings can be survived and that they will grow in resilience, i.e. develop a capacity to bounce back from painful experiences.

Developing this special knowledge about the messages behind the behaviour of children involves nurturing in oneself as a practitioner, a sensitivity to, and an understanding of:

- warm and nurturing relationships;
- vulnerability and resilience in children;
- the part emotion (affect) plays in the process of learning.

Warm and nurturing relationships

Video footage of newborn babies shows us that within minutes of birth they have the capacity to engage with others. Often referred to as a 'dance', what is striking about a newborn's ability, is the way in which he/she behaves and how they encourage spontaneous responses from others. For example, during feeding, babies suck and rest allowing pauses during which they gaze at their carer. These pauses are part of being social and are an invitation to engage emotionally whilst feeding and go beyond feeding being solely about physical nourishment.

The dance of dialogue

In other words, the soothing cuddle and soft reassuring tone of voice of an adult is the start of a two-way involvement, rooted in the pleasure of recognising 'I do this and you do that back'. A caregiver may then show their delight through an engaging tone of voice: 'Are we talking to each other? Yes, I can see you think so, too', said with a simultaneous smile of delight. We have described this in terms of attunement or being on the same wavelength as the baby. The baby will respond to such engagement with visible bodily delight which appears to run through ever fibre of their being, excited through nothing more or less than being in relationship and understood.

Knowing too when to recognise a baby's need to recover from experiences that may feel momentarily too much is also a part of caregiving. This can be observed, for example, in the simple game of 'peek a boo' (Tronick 1989). Young infants may find this game satisfying for a period of time but, intermittently, they may stop engaging briefly in order to gain some relief and to settle down physiologically. The attuned practitioner waits for the baby to 'come back on line' – 'Ah, hallo, here you are again, I wonder if you want to play some more now?' Shortly after, another short period of play may commence based on a dynamic interaction led by the cues from the careseeker. We can therefore see how jiggling a baby on the knee to satisfy the caregiver's needs for playfulness and not noticing the infant's response, may illustrate misattunement in terms of pace and rhythm.

However, this 'proto-conversation' (Trevarthen 1974) as described above is a dialogue that does not necessarily involve words. The dance is based on:

- a primary carer reflecting something back about *who* the baby is, namely a source of joy and love;
- a caregiver's attunement, which is about getting on the baby's wavelength and being deeply respectful of the baby's developing sense of self;
- a mutual pleasure in each other and the relationship developing empathy – 'You understand something of me and I understand something of you, together we have the beginnings of an understanding of each other'.

Figure 1.2 The dynamic interaction between careseeker and caregiver

The dance of dialogue when out of step

However, if we were to watch a severely depressed mother nursing her baby, we might see a dance that is out of step:

- The mother may not attend to the baby for long periods.
- The baby will try very hard to capture the carer's attention.
- The baby will give up, if after a great deal of effort, they are unable to gain the caregiver's care.
- The mother may suddenly seek engagement with the baby.
- If the mother is not responded to, she may intensify her need for contact in an manner that is out of tune with the baby.
- This may show itself by the mother bringing her face very close to the baby and demanding attention.
- The baby will pull away, in an effort to manage and down regulate the experience.
- There is a tensing in the baby's muscle tone, a pulling away of the neck and an averting of the gaze.
- The baby is communicating that the engagement is too much.

Why is it important to know something of these things as an Early Years practitioner? Just as mothers who feel overwhelmed by an infant's anxieties and frustrations will tend to respond erratically and so heighten the infant's distress we can see how this might find a parallel in the baby room of a nursery. We can see here how, if your baby and toddler rooms and reception classes are overly busy, with comings and goings, with sudden breaks in baby–carer connections, high turnovers of staff, or staff members being overly preoccupied with tasks, that babies will not experience a relaxed, natural rhythm to their day. Unintentionally, the staff will be like preoccupied and depressed mothers without enough time to enter the luxurious steps of the 'dance' and so enter into the dance on their terms only rather than being led by the music of the baby. It is of paramount importance, therefore, that secondary caregivers regulate their own anxieties:

> The depth of one's intimacy and feeling for others depends in part on the depth of feeling one experiences in ongoing relationships. Therefore not just any caregiver will do.
>
> (Brazleton and Greenspan 2000: 41)

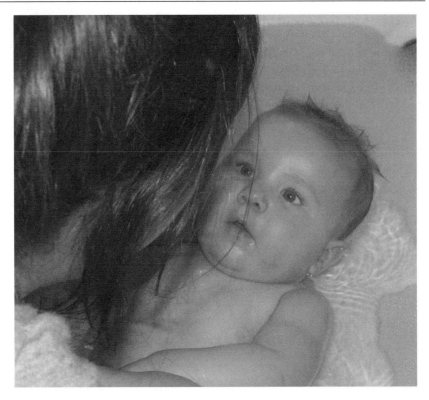

Figure 1.3 Babies signal at every level their need for closeness

Vulnerability and resilience in children

Infants are dependent on their carer for survival. In the early states of dependency when helplessness is felt babies signal at every level their need for closeness. Smiling, sucking, clinging and crying are all attachment behaviours that keep caregivers in close proximity so that love and care can be given and received. This memory of the gentle ebb and flow of care at moments of vulnerability becomes laid down and stored within each of us to be called upon to provide us with a sense of inner security at moments of anxiety and fear. This capacity to internalise feelings means taking inside a good enough experience of care and having the capacity to imagine a good enough experience of caregiving at times of uncertainty.

So, as an Early Years practitioner it is important that you are able to tolerate neediness, helplessness and vulnerability in others and attend to it. When Khalid stands at the gate alone, or wanders aimlessly around the room, he needs you close by, attending to his loss and by your reassuring presence offering hope that his feelings of distress will not last indefinitely. By responding promptly and accurately, and by offering comfort, you are signalling that you will not 'drop' him emotionally. What does this mean? Just as physically dropping a baby would have potential dangers so allowing a baby to 'fall from your mind' is putting very young children at risk.

Let us think about the first occasion when in your setting the time comes for a mother actually to leave her child for the first time. I wonder what your experiences of these partings have been like? Elinor Goldschmied writes so beautifully of the resources the key person for the child must draw on from within themselves at these times. The mutual support of colleagues at these times, too, can offer a great deal if everyone is of one mind about what it really means for a child to experience separation:

> The worker needs to find the confidence to listen to this quite appropriate crying and not try to hush it up or distract the child by waving a toy at him, making supposedly comforting noises or jiggling him up and down in her arms. Distress needs to be expressed in a context of quiet acceptance, in the way that we would try to comfort an adult experiencing loss and grief.
>
> (Goldschmied and Jackson 1994: 52)

Quiet acceptance of the message behind children's behaviour when embraced by an individual key person and the whole team, offers young children an important experience, of something shared within the group and a sense of being not only held safely by another person but within the arms of a community.

When a child's needs are met promptly and appropriately and at points of separation with sensitivity, tenderness and intimacy, then an inner strength develops. This capacity to adapt to future life experiences and to bounce back in the face of future challenges is called resilience.

Factors which might prevent the development of resilience

Of course, each of us will be able to think of examples of children who have developed resilience despite a substantial trauma or setbacks in their lives and who come through seemingly unscathed. The consequences of a weak attachment on children are evident in later relationships and the barriers they create to allowing positive engagement with others and subsequent healing. There are clearly protective factors for children and no one isolated stress will necessarily have long-term effects.

There is a range of factors that can adversely affect children's personal, social and emotional development. The following can all have an impact:

- premature/low birth weight
- poor health
- poverty
- lack of warmth and affection
- parental drug and substance abuse
- poor housing
- abuse
- social, racial or cultural discrimination
- poor relationships with practitioners.

Practitioners alone cannot counter all of these factors but they can make a huge difference by the way they work with young children and their families.
(SEAD – Guidance for Practitioners Working in the Early Years Foundation Stage, DCSF 2008)

What emotional resilience looks like

It is important with the growth of pre-school provision that practitioners are aware of the importance of their role as one of a series of new relationships outside the home that are important to a child's capacity to develop resilience. Key attachment relationships help children make sense of their experience, develop insight and understanding as new experiences present themselves and create a sense of inner safety to face new challenges. We will discuss the role of the key person in more detail in Chapter 4 – Positive relationships.

Resilience is built in children when they have had good enough experiences of:

- losing themselves happily in activities alone or with others;
- being able to talk about themselves and share some of what they feel inside as their language skills develop – emotional literacy;
- expressing aspects of themselves, through activities such as singing, movement, painting and other expressive arts;
- developing a growing contentment in their own company and according to their age be absorbed in tasks for substantial periods of time;
- developing a sense of themselves, which eventually allows them to join a group and not feel overwhelmed by others but connected to them.

Social connectedness to others comes as a result of having had an experience of nurturing involvement and engagement with another, which allows one to trust in the world:

> The evidence is unequivocal that experiences at all ages have an impact. However, it may be that the first few years do have a special importance for bond formation and social development.
>
> (Rutter 1981: 217)

Emotion, learning and the facilitation of attachment experiences

An attachment perspective can be very helpful to Early Years staff not only in their role as a carer but in their role as an educator. When young children are secure enough to explore objects in the outside world in the presence of a reassuring adult, they are able to be curious, explore and think. Unfamiliar situations and people may therefore be tolerated where there is enjoyment and security, leaving young children free to engage and be absorbed during exploration/learning. We might say that anxiety can prevent learning yet also that the right amount of anxiety is necessary to start learning, as in the phrase 'anxious or eager to learn'. It is important to bear this in mind when external learning goals are being set, such as at the end of the Early Years Foundation Stage. Practitioners who are mindful of the emotional and social aspects of the teaching and learning experience are better prepared to assist children on their journey towards such goals. When young children are unable to manage their feelings, develop resilience in the face of setbacks and do not trust the people around them, then their learning will be held back.

> Sustained shared thinking can only happen when there are responsive trusting relationships between adults and children.
>
> (SEAD, DCSF 2008: 42)

We will discuss this further in Chapter 6 – Learning and development.

Daily observation which is consistent, in-depth and meaningful:

- helps practitioners make sense of the enjoyment in the engagement between caregivers and careseekers, and of the feelings of loss expressed through unexpected separations;
- informs our thinking about what children are communicating through non-verbal communication;

- guides reflective practice and the choice of language used by practitioners to enhance their remaining open to hearing and seeing children's cues when seeking care;
- identifies at different developmental stages that attachment is a lifelong process and helps us to put our understanding of how children respond to change to good use.

How to make a positive contribution to good practice

- Put observational work at the heart of your daily practice and invite colleagues to the baby room, regardless of the age range they care for, to participate in regular infant observation sessions.
- Make these observations special events, with the observer having no responsibility for the care of the babies they are observing other than to observe.
- Suggest new staff follow the developmental changes of one baby over a 6-months period by writing an in-depth diary of their reflections and observations (as above).
- Meet in groups simply to share what you have observed without any requirement to make an assessment.
- Welcome curiosity about anything written on childhood and have a 'Book Club' (novels, autobiographies and articles) and give 30 minutes over to discussing these readings monthly at staff meetings.
- Introduce the Robertsons' films (see at the end of this section) as part of an induction for new staff.
- Teachers in reception classes might like to think about suspending whole-class teaching during the first week at school and make teaching children in small groups a priority. By being in close proximity to these children, and really getting to know them, you are building trust and saying: 'I am the new person in your life called your teacher. By really getting to know each other we can set off on this exciting new learning journey together.'
- Reception class teachers can help children by having a heightened awareness and understanding of each child's unique experience of loss, be it separation from parents or for those who have been in long-term group day care from the key people with whom they have built special and close relationships within that setting.

Your personal reflections

- Who attended to you when you fell or hurt yourself as a child?
- What helped or hindered your ability to recover?
- What led you into this work in the first place?
- What happens, when like John Bowlby, your views on child development differ from your colleagues?

Links to the EYFS

From the EYFS Practice Guidance. Personal, Social and Emotional Development – Making Relationships, p. 30

Look, listen and note

Birth to 11 months

- The sounds and facial expressions young babies make in response to affectionate attention from their parent or key person.
- Ways in which young babies respond to, or mimic, their key person's facial expressions.

8–20 months

- The skills that babies use to make contact, such as making eye contact, inclining their heads, wiggling their toes, smiling, vocalising or banging.

16–26 months

- How children look to others to check the acceptability of their actions.
- The different way in which young children show their concern for other children.

22–36 months

- The strategies children use to join in play with individual children or groups of children.

30–50 months

- Ways in which children show that they feel safe and cared for.

- Children who like to be with others, and those who need support to join in.
- Children's strategies for change.

40–60+ months

- Children's acceptance that they may need to wait for something or to share things.
- Children's relationships with other children and with adults.

Links to the Early Years National Strategy – Social and Emotional Aspects of Development (SEAD)

From SEAD Guidance for Practitioners Working in the EYFS

A Unique Child 2.1b

Learning points, p.16

Young children need to feel safe and secure. We can facilitate this by:

- considering the possible threats for each child and minimising these threats as far as possible;
- ensuring that the child feels safe both physically and emotionally;
- providing children with territorial space , for example, their own sleep mat, peg;
- helping them feel that they belong by having routines and rituals, for examples, welcome and departure songs and greetings;
- helping children to label and recognise their feelings;
- helping children learn strategies to calm down, for example, simple relaxation;
- helping children to cope with their fears and anxieties.

Using Bowlby's own research as a teaching tool to develop an understanding of attachment experiences

The Robertsons' Film: Young Children in Brief Separation – John (Concord Video and Film Council Ltd)

Joyce and James Robertson worked with Bowlby and made a series of films which recorded the reactions of children separated from their mothers when in hospital or during other separations such as fostering or a stay in a residential nursery. The Robertsons' research eventually changed paediatric practice in the United Kingdom. Today parents are actively encouraged to nurse and care for their children in hospital and visiting hours are unrestricted. Such sensitive and familiar care is believed to aid the healing process.

Showing the Robertsons' film to Early Years staff can help them:

- develop their observation skills;
- have a rare opportunity to conduct a 40-minute observation (allowing for regular pauses for group discussion);
- grasp the whole picture of a child's experience over a given period of time;
- reflect on current practice in their settings.

Description of the film

John has been taken to a residential nursery in the middle of the night due to his mother going into labour with her second child. John's father does not become the substitute carer as he has to work and there is no extended family able to care for him.

The film footage shows John from his first morning, waking in the strange and new setting, to the ninth day when he is reunited with his mother. Studying this film over many months, with different groups of Early Years staff, together we have been able to observe John's distress upon separation and identify together the phases of protest, despair and detachment.

Observation points

Below are some of the observations staff might make when shown the film, which highlight how the key principles of attachment can be understood through sensitive observation. Make sure all of these points are covered by the participants of the discussion groups:

- John wants to make a relationship with an adult carer and makes a lot of effort to do so.
- He is looking for a substitute mother.
- The other children in the nursery have been fostered and have not had meaningful attachments in their lives and are used to the lack of sensitive care.

- John is an only child and suddenly part of a big, noisy family.
- He starts off making attempts to play but is on the edge of the group.
- He sees too many carers across the first day.
- As soon as he attaches to a carer, she is gone as there are new staff on duty.
- John learns to get attention like the others by pushing himself forward and protesting.
- He shows in his non-verbal cues that he is overwhelmed, he sucks his thumb and tugs at his ear.
- John refuses to eat, is sick and develops a cold but there are no obvious signs of a temperature – 'It's as if his body is giving up.'
- He cries inconsolably and cannot be soothed and is desperate for contact with an adult.
- He seeks comfort in soft teddy bears and his soft blanket and even goes to be close to the observer (Joyce Robertson) for she at least offers constancy and consistency in her role from day to day.
- John turns his back on the group and lacks any liveliness in his manner or body tone.
- He shows by going to the door and getting his shoes that he knows what he needs – to go home.
- As the days pass, he appears not to recognise or respond to his father when he visits.
- He is distressed by his mother's return.
- He does not seem to be able to trust her and does not show any sense of joy at being reunited.

In Bowlby's own words:

> All the cuddling and playing, the intimacies of suckling by which a child learns the comfort of his mother's body, the rituals of washing and dressing by which through her pride and tenderness towards his little limbs he learns the values of his own, all these he has been lacking.
>
> (Bowlby *et al.* 1952, cited in Holmes 1993: 40)

When showing this film many staff become thoughtful about:

- the kinds of relationships they wish to build with children;
- the conflicts they feel during their busy, demanding days;

- their concern about the things that take them away from what they know matters; making relationships with the very young;

- the differences between a task-led and child-led environment;

- how practical solutions within the context do exist to some of the difficult behaviour practitioners manage on a daily basis;

- how looking after the emotional and psychological needs of children is often 'invisible' work and is sometimes not regarded as 'real' work;

- how intuitive caring can sometimes be overridden by routines and paperwork.

By observing their 1960s colleagues who were subject to the social, cultural and political experiences of the time, staff are able to learn about their own responses to working with children in the current childcare climate.

CHAPTER 2

The strange situation

Understanding about secure and insecure attachments

A practitioner's account

Ellie aged 3 years cannot lose herself in activity.

Ellie is three years old and goes to her pre-school every morning. She has become close to one particular member of staff, Clare, who is not her key person. Her key person has responsibility for several other children as well and is only in three mornings a week. This strong attachment to Clare in preference to her key person is something that feels too difficult for Clare to talk about in the staff team. There is not enough flexibility in the setting for there to be a change of key person. Clare does not feel it is her role to develop a special relationship with Ellie's mother, for fear of stepping on her colleague's toes. During one particular morning Ellie has started to do some painting, having held Clare's hand for the first ten minutes of the session. When Clare gets up from the table and walks to the kitchen to check the snack arrangements for later on, Ellie's eyes follow her. She puts down her paint brush and rushes to her side: 'Where are you going? What are you doing?' Clare reassures her she is just checking everything is in ready for the morning snack. 'I can help you', Ellie offers. Clare thanks her and gently guides her back to her painting. A few minutes later, a flustered parent arrives late, with one of Clare's key children, explaining the reasons for their lateness. Clare goes across to greet her. Ellie is by her side again asking: 'What happened? Why is Alex late?' This is typical of Ellie, who seems to watch every coming and going in the setting and needs to unexpectedly enter into conversations between adults as if they are her equals. As Clare describes this experience of being with Ellie, she says that she feels increasingly jumpy inside when she is with her and 'tied' to her. It is rare for Ellie to lose herself in any activity and her demands for Clare's attention leave this practitioner feeling both annoyed and guilty as she is unable to engage fully with other children.

The work of Mary Ainsworth from 1969 onwards has lead to numerous studies since then focusing on how children respond to being separated from their primary caregivers and how they behaved when reunited (Ainsworth *et al.* 1978). I am going to describe a simplified version of a strange situation test, but you may wish to read in greater depth about the original 'Strange Situation Test', a protocol which consisted of eight episodes. You will probably find you have some further thoughts about Ellie's situation, too.

You will, by the end of this chapter be familiar with four attachment styles and the parenting styles that may bring them about:

- secure
- insecure/ambivalent
- insecure/avoidant
- disorganised.

The strange situation test

If we were to invite a parent and child of 12 months to play with the toys provided in a laboratory/playroom and then ask the carer to quietly leave the room for a brief period of time and then return again, there are four types of response an observer might see according to the child's attachment style.

1 Attachment style of a securely attached child

This child's primary caregiver has been sensitively attuned to the child from birth and when distressed has offered comfort promptly and appropriately (Brisch 2002). The parent has had the ability to imagine the child's situation and respond promptly to their communications. This parent has also been quietly absorbed in observing their child at play and when she has noticed their interest waning, has offered some attuned involvement to gently re-engage the child.

When the parent in the test situation leaves the room at this point of transition, the child's need for care is heightened. The child may:

- follow after the caregiver and stand at the door;
- cry;

Figure 2.1 Attuned involvement to gently engage children in their learning

- show happiness and relief upon their return;
- seek physical contact in order to receive comfort;
- calm down and settle again to play before very long.

Later in life these children are likely to be:

- confident and empathic;
- naturally curious and enjoy exploration;
- able to move more successfully from a state of dependence to independence;
- positive in their outlook, for they trust in the world.

2 Attachment style of an insecure/ambivalently attached child

This child may have experienced their caregiver's communications as being uncertain and anxious. She may not be sure whether her requests for care will be met. The caregiver has not encouraged trust or exploration in the child and has found it difficult to be spontaneously tender.

When the caregiver in the test leaves the room and the careseeking system in the child is activated:

- the child will be very distressed at the point of separation and cry intensely;
- upon return the child will not be easily calmed;
- when picked up they will give confusing messages whether they want care, e.g. may kick, push, hit or turn away;
- it will be difficult for this child to settle and return to play;
- this child will continue to be very vigilant and check for the parent's whereabouts regularly.

Later in life these children are likely to:

- find it harder to be independent;
- be unable to become absorbed in play, for they are always checking the whereabouts of their caregiver;
- as their language abilities develop, use language skilfully to keep control in uncertain situations.

3 Attachment style of an insecure/avoidantly attached child

This child has not had an experience of an adult being on their wavelength. There has been misattunement at the times when they have sought care. The caregiver may have lacked warmth and empathy at times of sadness and distress. There might have been little spontaneous play, sharing of interests and inconsistent responses during joint activity. The parent may attend to their own emotions rather than the child's, leaving the child to take care of and organise their own feelings (Cooper *et al.* 1998).

When the carer in the test leaves the room and the child's need for care is heightened, the child may:

- show few visible signs of distress upon separation;
- show upon close examination, a raised heart rate and raised cortisol levels (a stress hormone);
- follow the caregiver's departure with their eyes (Brisch 2002);

- carry on playing but in a more distracted manner;
- not seek physical contact upon return of the parent.

Later in life these children are likely to be:

- unable to communicate what they need at an emotional level;
- managing uncertainty by keeping others at a distance;
- less able to ask for help when involved in educational activity.

4 Attachment style of an insecure/disorganised child

Currently these children are the focus of a number of education, health and social care early intervention initiatives. These children may come to your nursery with identified child protection concerns and in need of very sensitive support and care. Their early lives have been chaotic. Caregivers may have:

- communicated their own trauma to the infant;
- suffered from severe mental health problems;
- been responsible for severe physical and emotional neglect towards their dependent children;
- struggled with addictive behaviours;
- in a variety of ways, appeared frightening to their children.

When the carer leaves the test room and the careseeking system is activated, what is observed is very distressing. The child may:

- show a series of confusing and erratic responses to being separated;
- upon the return of the parent, run towards the caregiver and then away;
- freeze and stand perfectly still for long periods of time;
- display anxious behaviour like rocking.

Later in life those children who have not received skilled therapeutic early intervention:

- lack any capacity to manage stress or impulsive behaviour;
- may deal with their helplessness by attempting to control situations and people;

- feel worthless;
- find adults in authority potentially frightening;
- use fight/flight strategies excessively as they face difficult situations with no choice;
- are hypervigilant;
- are unable to distinguish different kinds of relationship so do not understand about distance and closeness;
- are more likely to be on the fringes of society and slip into criminal activity.

Using this knowledge in childcare settings

In order to summarise the value and importance of these findings for Early Years practitioners, I shall offer a few thoughts about how you can use this knowledge in the best interests of children in your care:

- Children who come into Early Years settings who are securely attached need to continue to experience an optimum level of support and nurturing care – this is best achieved amongst other things through the key person approach (see Chapter 4).
- Staff who have specific responsibility for babies should receive adequate training in how to facilitate warm, empathic attunement, for attachment at this stage is still 'work in progress'.
- Children who show insecure avoidant attachment behaviour need help building relationships and by offering reassurance on a daily basis they may develop enough trust to risk seeking care, and begin to believe their needs will be understood and they will not be rejected.
- Children with insecure ambivalent attachment behaviour need confident, consistent and predictable care, with warnings about unexpected changes and certainty that the adult is holding them 'in mind', thus leaving them calm and secure enough to explore the external world.

Ainsworth's research can help us think about what we may observe in children, and help guide our thinking and offer a frame of reference to anticipate what a child might need at any given moment. It is intended that Ainsworth's findings should provide us with a framework for thinking about how young children adapt to separation and any labelling of children should be avoided at all costs.

How might we think about Ellie in the light of this knowledge?

Let us see if we can understand something of what Clare was feeling at the beginning of the chapter and see if in any way she was holding some of Ellie's feelings that she could not manage for herself. In other words Clare's uncertainty might mirror Ellie's own fears in the setting about getting things wrong and feeling too insecure to move around the room securely and share with her peers. Might it be that Clare finding the capacity to share her worries with her colleagues or request taking on the role of key person to Ellie may be a way of relieving her of her own anxieties and attending to Ellie more fully? Anxiously attached children have often been in touch with parental anxiety from an early age and here again Ellie may feel at home with Clare because she is another adult struggling with being spontaneous – this is an experience she knows and is familiar with. It is Clare's role not to compound these past experiences but confound them by offering Ellie a different experience and being able to attend to her more fully. This might require her addressing the different beliefs about what the role of the key person really means for staff in her setting and through staff gaining clarity, offering Ellie greater security.

Attaching to a new social setting: the need for attachment and the desire to explore

How do you feel when you walk into a room full of strangers for the first time? Have you ever had the experience of arriving somewhere new, uncertain of what to expect? Remembering how you felt and how you coped with this situation is very important knowledge to acquire as a practitioner.

If you think about what it is like for an infant or toddler who starts to go to a childminder, whose place of work is also a home, you have an enabling environment which may be fairly close to a child's experience of home. Children entering child group care have a different set of challenges:

- getting to know several different adults;
- getting to know a fairly large group of other children;
- getting to know a place/space which is not a home and may or may not feel homely to the child.

This is a challenging social experience and involves different degrees of anxiety according to a child's previous experiences of belonging. It is not unusual for children who seem as though they have eventually settled to experience periods of unsettledness from time to time. Practitioners need to be alongside children at these times and offer quiet understanding until they are better able to cope again.

Transition within the same setting

Where settings are in different rooms and on different floors, helping children make a successful transition to a new room can take on great significance for all involved and requires thoughtful planning. For example, moving from the baby room to the 'toddler' room is an experience of losing a familiar place and important people again. Going upstairs to a new room can be like crossing a border into a new country for some children. The child may be thinking: How will my needs be met in this new and strange place? Where is my secure base in this group? What has happened to all the stability and familiarity I have known? How long is this experience going to last? Why can't I go back to where I felt happy and settled?

Preparation at the start of the day

Early morning in any group childcare setting is a potentially busy time with all the comings and goings. We live in a world of rush and 'must dash'! Parents are meeting schedules, you are busy getting the day underway and so both parties can get into this reciprocal 'busyness'. It is worth giving some thought to how one can actively take control of this time of day and make this point of entry a haven of peacefulness as you receive children into your care? Do staff meetings take precedence over preparing the setting? What would it mean to make the manner in which children are received each day an absolute priority? Certainly, parents will sense an attentive, thoughtful atmosphere when staff are not preoccupied and in a rush. For parents too, like their children, bring their careseeking system to your front door and require to be attended to calmly.

Preparing the setting means being aware that administration tasks have a dynamic quality. This means going beyond the routines of the morning, as being merely routine, and being mindful and watchful so each day begins afresh:

- calmly being mindful of the preparation of your room;
- allowing adequate time to organise the practical arrangement of the room;

- attending to the lighting inside the room by noticing what kind of a day it is outside;

- thinking about the temperature of the room;

- looking after the boundary between your room and the rest of the setting by working closely with any administrative staff, who may act as 'gate keepers' of the setting;

- sharing information thoughtfully with these key staff about any important parent visits or phone calls expected, so ensuring that those contacting the setting are anticipated, and greeted warmly.

Like the conductor of an orchestra it is important to stand poised, look around the space you have created and know when you are ready to conduct the events of the day, by being prepared both 'inside' yourself and within the emotional environment you have created to greet your children and parents with a containing calmness. Think about how you respond differently to fathers who bring their children to pre-school. Consider how they might feel about entering a predominantly female environment.

Second chance learning

For children with an attachment difficulty, entering any new situation presents very particular challenges. Practitioners through careful observation can attune to infants and young children with insecure attachment styles as they prepare for new transitions. Through empathy it is possible to offer more vulnerable children a 'second chance learning' experience (Winnicott 1965). This means there is an opportunity to provide a new experience of consistent care through sensitive caregiving. It is important to acknowledge too that a child who is securely attached who joins a setting where there is not sensitive attunement from staff can develop an insecure attachment style as a means of coping with an unpredictable and inconsistent environment.

Attaching to babies aged 3–12 months

All practice with this age range should be focused on getting to know a baby intimately by:

- making home visits first wherever possible;

- learning about the intimate care routines the mother has established;

- observing the unique nature of each carer–child relationship;

- communicating through touching, rocking, holding and talking;
- noticing how your facial attunement to the baby affects the baby's attention, brightness of expression and gaze;
- offering a rhythm to your speech in response to the baby's innate sociability;
- responding to the sucking and pausing pattern during feeding and letting the baby lead the way in this 'dance' and trusting a child-led interaction.

It may be the case that some very young babies today, amid the chaos of a busy morning at home, do not have a lot of close bodily contact upon waking. It may even be possible that some babies, whose caregivers are very rushed in the morning, may lift their babies from their cots, dress them hurriedly, feed them as they sit in a rocking cradle, put them into a car seat and then drive them to their destination. Some babies may even be handed over to a practitioner for convenience whilst still in the car seat.

Your first priority

Take the baby up into your arms and offer soothing comfort and bodily closeness as if you are restarting the day. Take the baby to the window and

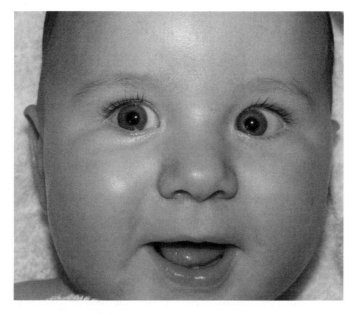

Figure 2.2 Attuning to baby's brightness of expression and gaze

speak reassuringly about the new day beginning and through the tone of your voice imitate the sort of rituals a mother who might have more time first thing in the morning would naturally go through. 'Did you sleep well? Here we are again, a new day is beginning and outside everything is waking up like you ….' Your tone of voice will influence a baby's capacity to relax, for it is through touch, warmth, sucking and rocking that a sense of well-being and calmness develops. Hormones released in the baby through nurturing in this way are important in the management of stress.

Practitioners who gather sensitively an understanding of a baby's familiar primary care needs such as sleeping, resting and feeding are working in real partnership with parents:

- Thoughtful discussion with parents about how they like to feed their babies will help you get beyond the practicalities of the feeding and gain some experience of the feeding relationship.

- Actively encouraging mothers who are still breast feeding to express breast milk for bottle feeding at the nursery can help dispel the myth that many mothers have, that they *ought* to wean their babies in preparation for going to nursery.

- Create quiet places for feeding so that the intimate care you wish to achieve is possible and this does involve sitting in comfortable chairs that support the back.

- Remember that you convey much about your own state of mind and body when feeding and so making sure you are comfortable when feeding is a priority – this does not mean sitting against a radiator on a hard floor.

- Discuss regularly with colleagues how you manage the demands of several babies in your care, if they are all unsettled at the same time.

- Make it a priority to perform as a key person all the intimate tasks of feeding, changing nappies and settling down before sleep.

- Nurture another member of staff in the care of your special children so they can confidently stand in your absence, with some authentic knowledge of the child being cared for (see Chapter 4 – Positive relationships).

Attaching to infants aged from 12 months onwards

The attachment behaviours we discussed earlier in the chapter will be more established by this age. You may even by means of thoughtful observation begin to see how a child's attachment system is activated and so by attending to their needs act as a protective factor against further insecure attachment behaviours becoming established. It is *never* the intention that any labelling of children should take place but it is very helpful to be able to read a child's affect signals. What I mean by this is being able to have an emotional map in your mind, to guide your understanding of each child's emotional response to separation and attachment.

The start of the day – finding a secure base

It can be really interesting to do a group observation over a considerable period of time and gain insight into how toddlers and reception class children actually pass from their parents 'arms' through the gateway to you. In her excellent book *Attachment in the Classroom* (Geddes 2006) shares an account of the start of a day in a playgroup observed at intervals over a year and revealing how different children manage transitions. Her in-depth observation is an invaluable resource for Early Years practitioners and reception class teachers from which to gain insight into how children create their own rituals to aid their passage from their primary caregivers to a secondary caregiving environment.

> Carla entered the transitional space and looked ahead into the play area. She mounted the slide and sat at the top, poised for descent. Minutes passed and she remained at the top of the slide staring ahead. Suddenly she swooshed down , walked into the play area and engaged with a worker at the table where an activity was laid out.
>
> (Geddes 2006: 85)

Valuing child-led experience as a part of creating an enabling environment encourages a constant reviewing of practice and regular self-evaluation. Curious and reflective practitioners will:

- be interested in seeing what the setting is like through a child's eyes;
- be interested in what children reveal through their non-verbal signals and how they deal in particular with the separation;
- notice how they feel at the start of each day as a practitioner;
- allow the space to reflect, think and check their emotional availability and so make authentic connections with each child.

Children with additional challenges at the point of separation

Children with additional challenges, because of experiences of instability in their earlier lives, require additional assistance.

Helping hesitant children attach to a play activity of their choice can be best achieved by having an intimate knowledge of a child's enthusiasms and anticipating their needs and preferences. The key person of a child with adequate language skills may find it helpful to 'wonder aloud' (Bomber 2007) when introducing them to a new activity, e.g. 'I wonder if you would like to have a quiet time with me and look at a story book this morning as everything may feel a little strange to begin with?' and gradually introduce a child to an activity with a lightness of touch, e.g. 'I remember yesterday you enjoyed playing in the sand pit, I wonder if you would enjoy ...'. Compare this with: 'Come along. What would you like to do?'

I hope the reader is able to go back in their mind to the beginning of the book and remember the gaze between mother and baby in the 'dance' that gives shape to a relationship that is full of pleasure and reassurance. When children do not have well-developed language skills, then practitioners need to be willing to answer subtle requests for attention, and a capacity to anticipate a child's need for comfort, holding exploration and discovery in an effort to increase a child's sense of security. The 'I wonder if ...' experience does not have to be spoken for it is about anticipating a child's need by standing in their shoes. Think of an ordinary occurrence like sitting next to somebody at dinner and their anticipating you might need the salt. By passing it to you, with a nod and smile there is a great sense of pleasure in the moment you were being thought about by another. This is so much more than just good manners, it is about somebody else's capacity to imagine you. Small acts of empathy can have a significant impact.

Partnership with parents

Working in partnership with parents to anticipate jointly their children's needs is an important bridge to build.

It can be rewarding for practitioners to help parents appreciate how they can be actively involved in establishing a secure base for their children before they arrive daily at nursery and can form part of the conversations about preparing for a baby/child's arrival. You might suggest the value to parents and colleagues of:

- getting up a little earlier in the morning to have some relaxing time with their children before leaving for nursery;

- forging a good relationship with parents so the child feels more secure during the hand over phase;

- planning with staff for a common and supportive approach towards each other through the sensitive handling of initial separations;

- deciding the appropriate periods of time for parental involvement in the settling in phase so as to lessen the chances of an insecurely attached child being in a heightened state of arousal at the point of departure;

- suggesting parents make some one-to-one time upon arrival home at the end of the day to re-establish a close bond.

Meeting the personal, social and emotional needs of parents in a professional capacity require practitioners to:

- attune to parents and see any vulnerability as an opportunity to strengthen;

- acknowledge through a culture of respect that parents are the first and most enduring educators;

- work in partnership with parents and have a positive impact on children's learning and development;

- understand that all parents have had differing experiences of education and place a different value on it;

- have a wide knowledge about services for families in the wider community and signpost parents to these when appropriate.

Building a secure base

Practitioners themselves help build a secure base in all the ways we have discussed and by being actively involved. By being sensitive and thoughtful practitioners can anticipate pre-school children's needs and offer solutions to unsettled behaviour by helping a child to 'organise their feelings' (Cooper *et al.* 1998). For example:

> I think you might be crying because you are too tired to eat your lunch after such an exciting and busy morning of play. I wonder if you might like to have a little rest before lunch tomorrow so that you can then enjoy lunch with your friends. I think we will try that tomorrow so you feel happier at lunchtime.

Developing children's emotional literacy through such explanations can help them with their capacity to articulate their emotional needs appropriately when they move into the larger group setting of a reception class.

When as a practitioner you allow your settings to be naturally what they are – opportunities for second chance learning experiences, unique spaces for play; both soothing and stimulating, full of sounds, smells, images and textures, stories, singing and dancing, fresh air and cosiness indoors – then there is the possibility for change and healing. You have so much potential for allowing a gentle rhythm to unfold each day and for small acts of kindness and care to be given and received. You possess, at arm's length, the capacity to offer peaceful encounters and a sense of being a part of a harmonious community for those who have known turbulence in their own families and communities at far too young an age. Your setting can be an Aladdin's Cave for those who have been fortunate to have a secure beginning. Try not to be distracted or overly anxious about curriculum changes, for what really matters is that you make a commitment to becoming a secure base for children and accompany them on their journeys and protect them when they feel overwhelmed. It is from such a place that learning and thinking can develop. Curriculum changes come and go but the inherent wisdom of children does not change.

At the beginning of the chapter we had a description of a practitioner, Clare, who was feeling jumpy inside and who had been adopted by Ellie as her key person. This did not allow her much time with the other children and made her feel awkward with her colleagues. In the light of this chapter, I hope a few thoughts about why Ellie might be so affected by comings and goings have begun to form, and why Clare might feel restricted in her practice and why the staff team are not discussing what might be happening in terms of Ellie's attachments to staff. Can you think about how you might help Clare with this difficulty now with your knowledge of different attachment styles?

How to make a positive contribution to good practice

- Constantly review the key phrases you use with children upon first meeting them.
- Discuss within your team how you offer different children reassurance, and how as a group of staff you manage separation anxiety and distress.

- Find opportunities to observe beginnings and endings of sessions.
- Become curious about the difference between a child who is healthily absorbed in play or activity and those who are avoidant and seeking safety in the task.
- Plan strategies for getting alongside these children and build a relationship through carefully chosen tasks.

Your personal reflections

- At what age did your first significant separation occur?
- What memories do you have of that experience?
- What strategies did you employ to help yourself with that loss of caregiving?
- Do you still find it useful to manage in the same way when you are confronted with the need to seek care?
- Think about something new you have recently started to do and use the feelings this experience has awoken in you as an opportunity to reflect on the very human emotions of fear and hope.

Links to the EYFS

From the EYFS Practice Guidance. Personal, Social and Emotional Development – Making Relationships, p. 30

Effective practice

Birth to 11 months

- Ensure that the key person is available to greet a young baby at the beginning of the session, and to hand them over to parents at the end of a session, so that the young baby is supported appropriately and communication with parents is maintained.
- Engage in playful interactions that encourage young babies to respond to, or mimic, adults.
- Ensure that all staff have detailed information about the home language experiences of all children.

46

8–20 months

- Follow the baby's lead by repeating vocalisations, mirroring movements and showing that you are 'fully listening'.

- Talk to babies about special people, such as their family members, for example grandparents.

16–26 months

- Give your full attention when young children look to you for a response.

- Help young children to label emotions such as sadness or happiness, by talking to them about their own feelings and those of others.

22–36 months

- Ensure that children have opportunities to join in. Help them to recognise and understand the rules for being with others, such as waiting for a turn.

30–50 months

- Establish routines with predictable sequences and events.

- Encourage children to choose to play with a variety of friends, so that everybody in the group experiences being included.

- Prepare children for changes that may occur in the routine.

40–60+ months

- Support children in linking openly and confidently with others, for example, to seek help or check information.

- Ensure that children and adults make opportunities to listen to each other and explain their actions.

- Be aware of and respond to the particular needs of children who are learning English as an additional language.

Links to the Early Years National Strategy – Social and Emotional Aspects of Development (SEAD)

From SEAD Guidance for Practitioners Working in the EYFS

A Unique Child 2.2, p.17

Children need adults to set a good example and give them opportunities for interaction with others so that they can develop positive ideas about themselves and others.

Before we can empathise with others, understand their feelings and see things from their point of view we have to understand three basic and important things:

1. Our feelings are important to us.

2. Other people have feelings.

3. Other people may think and feel differently from us.

Practitioners and parents can help children develop empathy by:

- encouraging secure attachments by meeting and greeting, getting to know each child and their parent, being available at the beginning and the end of the day, 'being tuned' to their needs and feelings;

- demonstrating active listening and modelling awareness of the feelings of others;

- encouraging children to listen to each other and notice each other's feelings;

- providing opportunities to develop the skills of empathy and modelling those skills themselves.

CHAPTER 3

A unique child

A practitioner's account

Peter aged 4 years is looking for a new secure base.

Peter is very special. He has moved recently to his reception class and is showing how unsettled he is by hurting other children and damaging the learning space when he is overwhelmed. He has been very settled in his nursery where he had been since nine months old and enjoyed a secure attachment to his key person. He is missing the intimacy of their safe relationship. Peter shows his loss when he is in assembly or sitting with his peer group on the carpet for the register or literacy and numeracy time. As if he fears he might be forgotten in the crowd, these are the times when he draws attention to himself by hitting other children, getting up and attacking toys and furniture. Following a series of serious attacks, Peter is at risk of exclusion from his new school. Staff, however, wish to prevent this and so bring some of the thinking from EYFS and his previous setting to their reception class. They appoint a key person for Peter and identify two other children who might benefit from this approach and set about nurturing this group through the transition. Peter has a social story each morning and at regular times across the day gathers with his key group to have a cosy time reading or sharing together. There is a school–home diary which allows for staff to work in partnership with parents and share and delight in positive news about Peter. Areas of difficulty are also regularly communicated so both sets of adults can help Peter in a consistent manner to organise his feelings when he feels overwhelmed. By the end of the first term Peter is much more settled and his outbursts have lessened and he is making friends.

In the previous two chapters we have seen how a number of different experiences shape each individual into the unique human being they are with 'their own characteristics and temperament' (EYFS Principles into Practice: Card 1.1 – A Unique Child – Child Development, DfES 2007b)

The first relationship that is exclusively devoted to the baby is that of the baby in relationship with their primary caregiver. We have discovered too, that a baby thrives upon the exchanges and nurture when this is a secure and intimate relationship. When there has been sensitive attunement, and the mother's smile brings about a smile from within the baby, this is the beginnings of a developing sense of self.

In order for the caregiver to offer a calm sensitive state of mind to the baby and enjoy this early relationship, there is also the need for the mother to feel supported through an attuned social network of doctors, nurses, health visitors, family and friends. What I mean by this is having a regular anti-natal nurse who gets to know a mother as a person, having a familiar midwife attend to her in labour, and having a connection to other new mothers in the early days and months of her transition into motherhood. These good attachments instil pride and value in mothering and support through reassurance and encouragement, the pleasure that can be taken in the baby by acknowledging that the process of mothering matters rather than seeing it as a task-led experience

When this unique child is given over into the care of a secondary attachment figure, such as yourself as an Early Years practitioner, then you, too, need to feel supported from within your network in order to fulfil the important role as a nurturer.

Nurturing the nurturers

Who nurtures the Early Years nurturers? Your professional body and colleagues help to support you as a secondary attachment figure by giving thought to safe and secure work practices. These include:

- sharing a common philosophy about putting children at the heart of the process;
- sensitive key carer approach to practice;
- safe adult–child ratios;
- space to discuss thoughtfully and reflect on your practice, e.g. via supervision.

Figure 3.1 The warmth of engagement through shared activity

Your role as nurturer of the baby/infant also involves taking care of the absent mother by holding her in your mind too. We have touched on this in the last chapter, by underlining the importance of all staff greeting and meeting parents warmly and sensitively. Parents who are clearly anxious may perhaps receive care and reassurance by staff more regularly than those who hand over their children quickly and rush off.

However, we are aware from the knowledge we have about different attachment behaviour, that parents who are seemingly matter of fact about dropping their children off at nursery by being in a rush or who may appear overly critical of staff, may be equally anxious about being separated from their children and this is their way of managing such a situation. Our avoidant parents may well be in a state of high distress as they drive away to work. Most parents at the point of handing over their children into the care of others will have their careseeking systems on high alert. It is through a culture of respect that different parental needs can be met most successfully too at partings and reunions.

The manner in which we are able as secondary attachment figures to do justice to this role depends on our capacity to continue to provide experiences, shaped to each child's unique qualities, which will increase the likelihood of their psychological and emotional growth. If as practitioner we feel overwhelmed or isolated, like struggling mothers do, our caregiving capacity shrinks and we then tend to apply a caregiving style that is about 'one size fits all'. It is therefore important to receive nourishment as a professional and regularly review your attachment relationship to your work.

Caregiving may be more important than previously thought

The unique repertoire that infants are born with, if attended to by good enough mothering, results in both emotional and cognitive growth. Neurologists are lucky enough now to have so many new tools and so much excellent equipment available to them that their knowledge about the brain is growing at an incredible rate.

If you are particularly interested in this field of study, you will find a section at the end of this book referring you to further reading. There are some bold and exciting claims being made about how a child's unique biology interacts with the environment and so alters the structure of the brain and its biochemisty. For the purposes of this book, I am going to leave the fine detail of these findings to the specialists who have begun to conduct these studies. I intend to continue to paint for you the broad picture of how we are shaped by what we experience in life.

Therefore, I wish to underscore the importance of human connections:

- We experience joy, hope and nourishment through feeling connected to others.

- The brain which we now know has plasticity is constantly changing and is shaped by all experience, but most positively through experiences of nurture, attentiveness, playfulness and curiosity on the part of the caregiver.

- Sensitivity to a baby's changing emotional states nurtures the emotional centres of the brain and helps a baby to make sense of what he/she is feeling and so helps them feel connected to the world around them.

- There is a connection between nurturing the social and emotional brain through sensitive attunement and young children being less vulnerable to psychological problems later in life.

- Consistent experiences of good feelings and connectedness are contagious and act as an immunity against future unreliable and unsettled times.

Neglect is devastating

One of the most distressing examples of disconnection and neglect was in the case of the Romanian orphans in the 1990s, when the world entered the disabling environments of thousands of children locked away in Romanian state institutions. The news footage of staring, rocking, traumatised children is etched in the memories of those who watched. It is sometimes important to remember that some young Early Years practitioners who were very young themselves when this event took place may have limited knowledge of this traumatic event. It is a stark yet important reminder, however, of the effects upon children who are deprived of affection, attention, stimulation and close loving relationships. The look in the eyes of those lost children said everything about how connectedness and nurture brings us alive, and how neglect destroys aliveness and hope.

Later studies of the brains of these children when scanned revealed how the frontal cortex, which is metabolically very active during a critical 2-year period in infancy, did not have the web of synapses (connections between nerve cells) expected, revealing 'black holes' in an area of the brain associated with social and emotional development. There before our eyes was what once had been an opinion, i.e. hard scientific evidence of the effects of despair.

The hope offered through secondary attachment figures

So let us see how naturally your work lends itself to a more hopeful process and meet Alfie, another child coming into an Early Years setting for the first time. Let us go back and journey with him on his first 12 months and look at some of the external environments that have influenced him and look at how early practitioners can share positively the next part of the journey with his parent, Stacey.

A practitioner's account

Alfie is one year old. His father left two months before his birth. His mother, Stacey, had not expected this to happen. She had been feeling socially isolated already, as she and her partner had set up home 10 miles from her family and did not know many people locally. At about the same time as

---

Alfie's father left, the small local hospital closed down and Stacey had to travel 7 miles by bus for her ante-natal appointments. She had really got to know well the midwife at the previous hospital and lost contact with her at this point. The nine months of hospital appointments were lonely experiences as Stacey saw a different nurse each time she had her check-ups, and she was sad that she had no partner to accompany her to the scans. On the night Stacey went into labour, she called a taxi and took herself to hospital. Fortunately the labour was fairly straightforward but what she remembers most about the experience was that there were so many changes of midwife that night. When her 19-year-old sister finally arrived to support her during labour, she was so pleased to see a familiar face. Three months after Alfie was born, Stacey's mother died and so four months ago she moved back home to live with her father and sister. Recently, she has suffered from depression, which is possibly linked to her mother's death, and her new GP has offered her medication and supported her wish to take up a job, so she can get out of the home during the week. Alfie is starting at his local children's centre three days a week. Stacey has been an attentive and loving mother but sometimes she says she has felt very sad over the last year and she is uncertain about her parenting skills. Currently, she is finding it hard to settle Alfie at bedtime.

A unique window of opportunity

Generally, the details of Stacey's journey so far would not be known to others. At this point however there is a window of opportunity for a good enough Early Years setting to offer a positive and supportive framework to Alfie and Stacey and to share in the next stage of this parent–child journey.

How? It is possible that in certain settings the unique 12-month journey that Stacey and Alfie have been on could be reduced to a label: single mother suffering from depression. It is important to reframe this in more positive terms by recognising Stacey has offered Alfie the best environment that she could during the nine months that she carried him. She was failed in her hope of finding an attachment figure to support her in her mothering during her pregnancy. The maternity services failed her at a point of profound emotional and physical stress – during her unique labour. She has given Alfie the best start in life she can by breastfeeding him for six months, through good skin to skin contact and by giving a gentle rhythm to their days and maintaining a closeness together. She has achieved much. She has left one community and moved back to another because she recognised the need for a supportive family. However, she does not feel very attached to the outside world because her family is still grieving. She has recognised her sadness and sought help because she felt some distance from her child in her grief and, in so doing, has made a good attachment to her GP.

What is your role? Quite simply:

- to cherish her child;
- to offer unconditional acceptance;
- to welcome any opportunity to work collaboratively with Stacey;
- to help support the needs of her unique child.

Stacey has successfully dealt with many challenges in the first 12 months of Alfie's life and now you are able to take an interest in Alfie's development and share your enthusiasm in his positive progress and in so doing make up for earlier lost opportunities with other professionals she has come into contact with. There are specific ways in which you can affirm mother and baby's uniqueness:

- through meaningful and warm daily dialogue;
- through recording Alfie's milestones in a way that celebrates his development as an individual;
- through linking Stacey up with any multi-professional support available for parents.

The main requirement of you as a practitioner who wishes to appreciate the uniqueness of each child, and parent for that matter, is to be open and generous in your thinking. As you prepare to receive a child into your care put on the widest lens you can and think deeply and widely about the child. Discuss with colleagues in advance your thoughts and feelings about building this new relationship. It is through your awareness of what you bring to the interaction with each child that you build on their existing experiences and by so doing you allow each child to flourish as an individual.

How to make a positive contribution to good practice

- Offer opportunities for children to express themselves through painting, singing, dressing up and so help them to develop a sense of safety, acceptance and their uniqueness through free expression.

- Encourage children to engage in open-ended imaginative activity within regular, relaxed and calm structured places, e.g. Treasure Basket activity for younger children and heuristic play for older children (see pp. 102–3).

- Involve children in your observations by writing them up as letters to the child celebrating their tangible and positive achievements.

- Offer small group activities to reception class children, who still need to be listened to, so they can express who they are and what they are doing rather than them losing their sense of self in the larger more formal whole-class teaching and learning situations.

- At the beginning and ending of the school term allow extra listening time for children to share in a meaningful way their own experiences outside school and connect them to their learning experiences in school so a child has a sense of wholeness about who they are.

Your personal reflections

- Think about your own experiences of entering a group situation.
- How do you hold on to a sense of who you are and how do you try to get your uniqueness across to others?
- What do you most want people to know about who you are?
- Who or what helps you to find that sense of safety to share aspects of yourself and your experience with others?

Links to the EYFS

A Unique Child

Principle: Every child is a competent learner from birth who is resilient, capable, confident and self-assured.

Figure 3.2 Offering children the opportunity to express themselves while listening attentively as a practitioner

Commitments

Child development

Babies and children develop in individual ways and at varying rates. Every area of development – physical, cognitive, linguistic, spiritual, social and emotional – is equally important.

Inclusive practice

The diversity of individuals and communities is valued and respected. No child or family is discriminated against.

Keeping safe

Young children are vulnerable, they develop resilience when their physical and psychological well-being is protected by adults.

Health and well-being

Children's health is an integral part of their emotional, mental, social, environmental and spiritual well-being and is supported by attention to these aspects.

From the EYFS Principles into Practice: Card 1.1 – A Unique Child – Child Development

Effective practice

- Understand the processes involved in babies' and children's growth, development and learning.

- Support babies and children to develop a positive sense of their identity and culture, this helps them to develop a positive self-image.

- Encourage, listen and respond to babies' and children's communications, both non-verbal and verbal.

- Acknowledge the different ways in which babies and children learn, and be aware that learning is a process that cannot be rushed.

- Recognise that babies' and children's attitudes and dispositions to learning are influenced by feedback from others.

Challenges and dilemmas

- Ensuring the needs of every child are fully met, even when temporarily you need to spend more time with a child who is new to the setting or whose behaviour is giving rise for concern.

- Keeping a focus on the child's needs when a parent also has significant needs.

- Maintaining records suitable for sharing with colleagues in an interagency team while acting as a point of contact for a child and their family.

Links to the Early Years National Strategy – Social and Emotional Aspects of Development (SEAD)

From SEAD Guidance for Practitioners Working in the EYFS

A Unique Child, p.12

A unique child requires practitioners to 'tune in' to children as unique individuals. This involves:

- knowing how children develop;
- observing children closely;

- listening actively, attentively, and with respect, to all children and parents whatever their background;
- being able to put yourself in the child's or parent's shoes by stepping outside yourself, and by the way your setting is run, and seeing things from their point of view – often called having empathy;
- valuing what you learn from observing children and from talking with parents and acting on it for the benefit of the children;
- understanding that physical and mental health and well-being are closely related.

CHAPTER 4

Positive relationships

Why the key person approach really matters

A practitioner's account

Oliver aged 2 years and 9 months has his first visit to nursery.

Oliver is on his visit to his new nursery. He is spending the morning in the company of the head of the nursery and being discreetly observed throughout the morning by the staff member who will eventually be his key person. His mother and the childminder are sitting to one side of the room watching him as he lifts down objects from various shelves and interacts with the adult with him. He is encouraged to put things back in their place before moving on to whatever catches his eye next. From time to time he looks over at his mother and the childminder and beams with pleasure at his own achievements. Some of the older children in the group offer small gestures of assistance and a few words are exchanged with the other children sitting around his table. At the end of the session, the head of the nursery has a discussion about Oliver with mum and the childminder so that he hears the positive observations she has made about his capabilities. He hands his piece of artwork over to his childminder with great pride and goes off to get his coat smiling happily. This has been a great success and a happy event for all. The setting has a feeling of calm purposefulness and the concentric circles of support, allowing Oliver to be at the heart of the process, are strongly felt yet barely visible. Everybody who matters to Oliver, in terms of his daily care up until this point, is present and everybody to be involved with his future care, exploration and discovery is there. Lots of pleasurable communication and involvement in this process provides a cradle of security for Oliver. Like the various objects on the shelves every part of Oliver's life has its place in this enabling environment on this special morning for him. The inner calmness and the thoughtful supportiveness that has gone into this new experience reveal what is possible in terms of seamless transitions.

The importance of transitional objects

In the previous chapters we have discovered the importance of close and warm relationships from birth, and the benefits for each unique child of feeling connected to their primary caregiver. We have begun to see how when children have an early experience of separation and have to adapt to strange or new situations they carry with them an awareness of something important missing. They seek at these times something that they can associate with that feeling of security and completeness. On a temporary basis young infants may seek a comforter, e.g. a soft blanket often termed a 'snuggly' or teddy bear to help them recreate a sense of comfort, well-being and an imagining of the missing relationship.

This is what Winnicott terms the transitional object. The baby, he says, is exploring a potential space, a 'me' and 'not me' space, as a solution to experiencing the beginnings of what will be later separateness. The 'snuggly' is the baby's creative response to this new experience. The object signifies a part of the 'not me' world yet is a reminder of mother. The tactile, soft object with the smell of the mother is used as if it is the mother.

When separations come too soon or are for long periods of time across a day, then it is very important that there is a great deal of thought given to how we can assist children in feeling attached to another significant adult, who shows an openness to fostering a close and intimate knowledge of the child.

The role of the key person

It is the intention of this chapter to bring together the thinking in the previous chapters and focus on an important aspect of Early Years practice: the role of the key person. This way of working is central to:

- successful new beginnings for babies and infants;
- developing resilience and managing new situations in the future;
- young children having their individual needs met;
- receiving appropriate care and understanding within a group;
- creating a unique relationship with a child and a family;
- offering a secure base from which to explore, become curious and learn.

When the key person approach is truly valued for what it can become for both children, practitioners and parents, then we see Attachment Theory in practice. For it is through this thoughtful way of working with a small

Figure 4.1 Fostering close and authentic relationships between practitioners and children

group of children, that staff have their best opportunity of conveying to a child that their inner emotional states are known and shared – *affect attunement*. Staff who are available, attentive and attuned to infants and young children help them at times of separation and loss.

Maintaining a sense of security

What does a key person approach mean from an attachment perspective?

- The setting becomes relationship-led rather than task-led.

- It is about building a special relationship with a small group of children and their families.

- When the child/adult ratios are at an optimum level, it is possible to hold each child in mind and to attune to their cues so their needs are met promptly and appropriately.

- Staff engaged in a key person approach are better able to develop a deep knowledge of the children in their care.

- When the day's routine values the importance of a secure base, there is a commitment to providing periods of calm and a 'coming together' in a safe place so children can 'refuel' emotionally.

- It offers security, continuity and familiarity for parents when they wish to talk with staff about their child.

- Transitions to different stages are able to be planned for with each child's individual needs in mind.

- When a practitioner's group of children feels warm, intimate and manageable then it is more likely that staff will seek professional support to think through issues relating to the care of their key children.

The difference between key person and key worker

When staff groups, most of whom have now adopted the title of key person rather than key worker as identified in the EYFS, explore what the change of title means to their practice, some express openly that it is yet another change of title. They are not altogether sure why the change of title matters. Others, when they have time to think together about the possibility of the title being changed for a reason and link it to what they have begun to understand about the importance of successful attachments, share some very interesting insights. Many practitioners express the view that 'worker' had been a job title. This usually meant having a set of administrative responsibilities, like keeping the child's file up to date. They have felt their care was more task-led. When we consider what difference the word 'person' makes to their role in the light of attachment thinking, they identify that it is more to do with people and relationships and that this is a potentially more satisfying role. The role that comes to the foreground is that of the importance of being in relationship with children set against a background of administrative tasks. This is an important distinction.

> Most of us have, or would like to have, a special relationship with some person on whom we can rely, a relationship which is significant to us. If we are parted from that person we have ways of preserving continuity even through long separations. We use telephones, letters, photographs, recollections, dreams and fantasies to keep alive the comfort that we derive from such human relationships. When we lose them, we experience sadness and often deep feelings of despair.
> (Goldschmied and Jackson 1994: 42)

The island of intimacy – Elinor Goldschmied

Elinor Goldschmied was very mindful of the importance of creating pauses across the day so that children could have time to gather themselves in and experience periods of calmness. She suggested that perhaps for 20 minutes before lunch, small groups of about four to five children had the undivided attention of their key person. The special quality of listening and the manner of the adult at these times offers an opportunity for contact, connection and sensitive communication.

Materials for the island of intimacy might include:

- postcards with pictures of animals or children;
- collections of buttons, shells or other varied small objects;
- purses, bags or boxes with objects inside them;
- small kaleidoscopes;
- pictures or objects related to the key person's own hobbies.

The important thing is that this time should be tranquil. Then, when the meal is ready, the key person goes to the table with their small group.

(Jackson 2009)

Our emotional well-being lies in these quiet, reflective times together or alone, when we have a deep sense of connectedness to ourselves, others alongside us, the wider world and life. Having opportunities at a young age to experience these special pauses may lead on to valuing and developing the capacity to allow ourselves to 'lie fallow' amid the otherwise busy lives of adulthood.

Intimacy and the key person

When the opportunity comes for a member of staff to take on such a special, nurturing relationship there is a window of opportunity to get to know a child intimately and to nurture a trusting relationship with an individual family. What do I mean by intimate? I mean being understood in a manner that is experienced as being loved and delighted in, for who you are, rather than for what you might be doing. Being known in this way is the most important way in which as a secondary attachment figure you can really build on the sense of self-worth that has already been laid down by a good enough primary caregiving relationship. There is no intention to take over the role of a parent but to offer a special secondary relationship during a significant period of separation. In the case of children who have not had stable and secure early attachments, by introducing a key person system, it is possible to offer an experience of 'second chance learning' (Winnicott 1965) by attending to and offering a child a new experience of how their emotional needs can be successfully met regardless of their previous experiences.

The example below demonstrates this idea of intimacy more clearly and the importance of developing the capacity to notice and know a child intimately from moment to moment, as the practitioner Teresa does with one of her key children, Thomas. In a manner similar to that of a parent, Teresa is developing an in-depth knowledge of Thomas and he trusts enough to know his non-verbal cues will be met.

Observing and recording the personal, social and emotional development in a narrative form as recorded below through meaningful in-depth accounts of primary care routine is 'look, listen and note' in action.

A practitioner's account

Thomas arrived at nursery for an early morning start. Mum talked with Teresa and explained that Thomas had an unsettled night and may be tired during the day. She also passed Teresa his special rabbit, a comforter from home, which travels with him every day. Later that morning Teresa noticed that Thomas was quieter than usual and seemed reluctant to explore the environment. When it was time to go outside Nikki collected the children's coats. Thomas immediately looked for Theresa and stretched his arms out towards her. Teresa noticed Thomas's non-verbal communication and she picked him up and smiled and said 'Come on Thomas, up you come would you like to go outside?' Thomas usually likes going outside but on this occasion he snuggled into Teresa's neck and began to twizzle his hair. 'Shall we find rabbit and then you can go to sleep?' asked Teresa, who had recognised that this was a familiar routine Thomas repeats before falling asleep. Thomas points towards the sleep area. Teresa settled Thomas in the cot, letting him hold her finger, which provided a comforting presence until he fell asleep.'

EYFS .Context for Learning: Care routines – Time for rest. Thomas 13months, Resource index at: www.standards.dcsf.gov.uk/eyfs/site/resource/

This is an example of a practitioner having the confidence to follow the child's lead and responding to the subtle cues for comfort and holding. The ease with which Thomas's needs were met comes from a deep knowledge of him as a unique child.

These learning journeys are of immense value to both practitioners and parents in the early weeks of starting in a new setting and demonstrate how feeding and sleeping routines can be shared creatively.

What are the obstacles to establishing a meaningful key person system?

Below are some of the difficulties practitioners identify when faced with the practicalities of developing an effective key person system.

The three key obstacles are:

1. time

2. paperwork

3. poor communication.

Further obstacles include:

- a high turnover of staff;

- staff absence due to sickness, holidays and maternity leave;

- staff/child ratios not being realistic;

- a lack of discussion amongst staff about the role of the key person;

- staff dynamics which reflect a lack of shared commitment or enthusiasm for a setting-wide approach and a reluctance to tackle issues relating to sensitive issues such as requests for change of staff and the flexibility to respond to this situation;

- an absence of parental interest, involvement or education about the benefits of the approach;

- parental anxiety about the special bond between staff and children;

- a lack of support for staff with the emotional demands of working in this way;

- the key person's own feelings.

What solutions can practitioners offer to ensure an effective key person approach?

- *Time* given to thinking and planning for a key person approach means there is an automatic emphasis upon giving time to being *with* children and structures in place that are *about* children and shared quiet times.

- *Paperwork* when it is timetabled into a week allows for a clear boundary between time given to children and the set time given to completing written tasks. Including children in the planning process combines both being with children and recording outcomes. Valuing high quality observation and record keeping that involves parents and children is a skilled, professional task and very rewarding because it is performed within the context of a relationship.

- *Communication* is key to a successful key person approach:
  - Making sure there is a special atmosphere at the beginning of each session provides a settling in time when parents can identify staff with their key group in a specific place (a secure base). Staff awareness of this provides security for both parents and children.
  - Making face-to-face communication a priority rather than an over-reliance on message boards allows staff to become sensitive to the changing 'mood' between parents and children at the beginning and ending of sessions.
  - A 'home-setting' diary allows for a daily flow of communication especially when multiple carers are delivering and collecting children.
  - Communication as a team that differs from an agenda-led staff meeting can lead to sensitive thinking about children, e.g. reflective practice staff groups and collaborative problem-solving groups which offer this finely tuned professional dialogue.
  - Rotas that maximise overlapping of key staff enable face-to-face contact when communicating about children.
  - A system like a nurses 'ward report' session by the early shift brings those coming on the late shift up-to-date with the important details of the day so far.
  - Having a 'buddy' system enables two staff to communicate regularly about the needs of their group of key children. This is good preparation for staff absences, e.g. training days or withdrawal from the setting on a temporary basis to complete written tasks. It can

be helpful for pairs of staff to take it in turns to sit quietly each day during coffee breaks or when it is story time or lunchtime and share in a key child discussion.

- *A high turnover of staff* can reflect a lack of job satisfaction and so developing practice that engages staff with children in a meaningful and satisfactory way, via a key person approach, may offer staff greater continuity in their working lives and make them feel part of a caring community.
  - ○ Staff who have such an opportunity to build close and secure relationships with their key children will plan for absences and be attuned to separation with a degree of sensitivity and thoughtfulness not present when it is just an extra job they do.

- When *staff–child ratios* are finely tuned to the reciprocal needs of the adult and child, then high quality care feels achievable. Ratios that are top heavy can lead to shortcuts in practice and a feeling of being overwhelmed.

- *Supervision* (see p. 84) can allow an important space for learning and growth as a practitioner and develop a greater awareness of one's reactions and responses to relationship building with children. Supervision can also offer a valuable source of emotional support for what is a demanding yet rewarding role, as well as discussing concerns about parental anxieties about the closeness of relationships with key carers.

- *Staff dynamics* can either foster or prevent this attuned way of working and views relating to dependency and independence, anxieties about becoming too attached and separating from children, as well as worries about parental feelings about the establishing of special bonds, should be discussed in regular supervision.

- *Educating parents* about the key person approach can be through:
  - ○ having a clear statement of intent in a brochure or prospectus;
  - ○ visual displays in the setting with photographs and creative statements about what you are proud of in terms of the key person approach you have created as a team;
  - ○ sharing your thinking about the approach with enthusiasm through open days, evenings and during initial nursery visits;
  - ○ making home visits as a first step in the preparation process for children's arrival in the setting.

Building bridges between home and the setting

It can be very useful for practitioners to have an image of a bridge in their mind when building a partnership between home and the nursery. There is little value in keeping one world separate from the other and apart from a different physical setting both places may be seen as an extension of the other. When parents and practitioners stand on the bridge and children take the hand of each in turn, all parties from this position get a view over to the other side in terms of seeing across to each other's worlds. It can be helpful for practitioners from time to time to ask themselves where they are on the bridge – are they clearly visible to parents and can they see the child's home? What is meant by home is the child's ethnicity, culture, religion, home language and family background. Practitioners can help young children feel validated in terms of their self-image by knowing these connections exist to home and vice versa and forging these links may be through:

- introducing practitioners to young children within their natural home environment through home visits and so establishing an important point of reference in a child's mind, i.e. this person knows my family and is not a complete stranger to me;

- each child having their own accessible laminated book which includes photographs of family, grandparents, friends, pets and significant places and events to be used for reassurance and as a talking point according to child's language ability;

- a visual wall display showing the timetable across a day with the start point showing parents parting, with all the activities and routines in between and the end point being the coming back together. By being able to point to where a child is on that journey through a day can help begin to develop a concept of time and the length of separation;

- inviting parents to contribute regularly to activities and experience what their children experience by taking part in different kinds of play during parent evenings;

- having a favourite soft toy from the setting who goes home in turn on weekends, when parents are encouraged to keep a photographic record of teddy sitting, eating, sleeping and meeting other family members in the chosen child's home and later displaying the photos back in the nursery;

- each child could have a picture of staff and different favourite areas of the setting to have at home for cosy talking time with parents.

Issues relating to parental fear about practitioners replacing them in their absence and assuming too much significance in a child's life can be lessened by such genuine sharing and valuable knowledge of each other's worlds. When bridges are built between practitioners and parents in an atmosphere of mutual respect this has a positive impact on children's development and learning.

Some of the obstacles to setting up a meaningful key person approach are often symptoms of being uncertain about where to focus meaningfully one's efforts in the team as a whole. Deciding to adopt the approach offers a wonderful opportunity to review together what really matters in terms of practice, curriculum and communication. Like the encircling arms of a mother, managers need to create space for important inter-collegiate communications to develop how satisfying daily practice is and how valued and connected staff members feel to their work, the team as a whole and children and parents.

What meaning does the key person approach have in a reception class?

A practitioner's account

Robert, aged five years, does not expect anyone to 'hold him in mind'.

It is a Friday afternoon and I am sitting in the kitchen with five-year-old Robert. He has a tea tray balanced on his lap. This is his desk for today because the kitchen table and every other space is covered with the clutter of family life. I am teaching Robert in his home because he has been excluded from his reception class for a violent outburst and we are awaiting a new school placement for him. As we pack up our books and prepare to say goodbye, I ask him if he is doing anything special on the weekend. He tells me with real liveliness in his face, that he's going 'up town' with his Grandad to look around the shops. Noticing his aliveness and excited anticipation of this outing, I find a space inside me to carry this event, take care of it over the weekend and to find a minute to imagine Robert on his shopping trip.

When we meet again the following week, it is the first thing I ask him about: 'So, how was your shopping trip with Grandad?' Before he answers, he stares at me with a look of disbelief, which seems to say, 'You remembered that, you remembered about me?'

Through supervision this teacher was able to explore the meaning of this powerful interaction. Many children like Robert have grown up used to *not* being 'held' in another person's mind, in other words being 'dropped' from an adult's thoughts and with little expectation of being understood by another and so over time lessening their chances of being willing to understand other's points of view.

This exchange between Robert and his teacher has been a formative experience for the teacher. It has taught this particular teacher how powerful the face can be at any age as a source of communication and how important it is for teachers to develop the capacity to respond to a child's affect states, and that 'holding them in mind' really matters.

Reception class teachers and attachment thinking

There is real value in reception class teachers remembering this too, for they assume a potentially important place in a child's mind as another significant transition to school is made. Being 'held in mind' goes on for a long time after the end of special relationships. Recently some nursery practitioners were describing how because they shared a site with their primary school they would often have to pass the window of the reception classroom. If any of their former key children saw them they would rush to the window, wave furiously and beckon them in or hold their work up to the window. Waving back, staff described the disapproving looks of their school colleagues who ushered the children away from the window. This puzzled this group of practitioners for they felt they were having to deny an important connection and knowledge of these children and aroused in them their own sense of loss and the unnaturalness of the situation. They wondered why they had never been asked to visit and contribute to the early settling in period and why they were never asked for help when particularly vulnerable children were finding it difficult to settle. These are important questions to think about, for they offer possible opportunities for exciting collaborative working and extending the key person approach to reception class settings, to help with the bridging of transitions.

Supporting the transition to 'big' school

Reception class teachers have such a rich resource to learn from in terms of good Early Years practice in this area. Whether children are joining school from home or from a long-term or short-term placement in nurseries, teachers are facilitating an important transition and another 'new' beginning. Each child brings their own story of attachment, separation and area of sensitivity to new experiences. This can easily be forgotten in the business of organising a class of thirty children. A good working basic knowledge of Attachment Theory is as relevant at this stage of a child's life as any that has gone before. Children during the settling in period, rely on their sense perceptions of touch, taste, smell, seeing and their *affect* to guide them through the first few weeks. Each child is hoping that their class teachers will hold something special about them in mind across weekends and holidays to reassure them as they negotiate sharing their new teacher with thirty others. This is why so many children make strong attachments to the classroom assistant who often has extra time and space inside to hold and digest the unique details of individual children's lives, like the names of pets or noticing a new pair of shoes worn to school. Staff who attend to the attachment process as much as the curriculum content in these early stages understand the importance of not overwhelming children but making the Social and Emotional Aspects of Learning guidance (DCSF 2007) a living document at transition and beyond, reinforced by the SEAD materials (DCSF 2008). Let us look at some practical ways in which staff can become key people for reception age children and how a teacher's

Figure 4.2 Getting to know children in small groups actively builds trust and rapport

awareness of these preoccupations can provide security before the formal structures of the timetable dominate.

Practical ways to be a key person in the reception class

- Identifying children who are excessively anxious and working with classroom assistants to create cosiness in small groups at the beginning of the day is a reassuring start for these children.

- Encourage all staff to be predictable in their manner at the start of the day, i.e. waiting in the same place, with an air of being prepared and expectant. Staff who are dashing around doing last minute things or who have popped out of the classroom are like preoccupied mothers and this may signal concern for some children.

- Consider delaying too much whole-class teaching until staff have established bonds in small group activities and a level of trust has been built up. Why should any child immediately trust their class teacher to teach them? Learning is about managing anxiety and feeling secure enough to explore the world in the company and presence of others.

- Read social stories to those who continue to falter at the transition.

- Establish a set amount of time, e.g. one month, as a settling in period with an emphasis on routines that enhance attachment being valued, e.g. getting to know each other in circle time activities.

- Emphasise what is coming next in terms of routines and give clear warning about any change before it occurs.

- Remember that most of us regress slightly at points of significant change before moving forward again with confidence. Avoid creating a culture where phrases such as: 'You ought to be ... by now'; 'Come on you are a big boy now'; 'At big school we ...'.

- Teaching assistants should have knowledge of how to facilitate successful attachments with children and develop their observation skills at an individual and whole group level.

- Inviting experienced Early Years staff into your school to share their knowledge in this area is good multi-professional practice in action.

NB. For an in-depth article on this theme see Appendix 1 in SEAD Practitioners' Guide (Grenier *et al.* 2008: 49).

How to make a positive contribution to good practice

- Make it a priority that rotas reflect the ethos of your setting and put the importance of emotional security and well-being at the heart of your practice as part of an enabling process.

- Value the importance of a familiar and consistent voice and the pleasure of being with key children at times of intimate importance, such as nappy changing and feeding, where shared rituals can be relied upon rather than children being attended to by constantly changing adults.

- If you are reviewing your key person practice, visit other settings and see what they have learned from the experience and incorporate the best practice into your context.

- Invite reception class staff and primary school headteachers into your nursery to read stories or to facilitate an activity so they become familiar faces.

- Offer a member of staff to assist in reception classes in the first few weeks of term, even if it is only for an hour per week.

- If reception class teachers identify very vulnerable children with specific attachment difficulties contact the Nurture Group Network (info@nurturegroups.org) for advice on good attachment practice in primary schools. Of particular use is the Boxall Profile, a tool to assess the specific needs of vulnerable children with attachment difficulties.

- Invite a cluster of schools and Early Years settings to sponsor one member of staff to train towards the Nurture Group Network Certificate so the locality has a resource to call upon for advice with vulnerable children.

Your personal reflections

- Who do you turn to for comfort, guidance and protection personally and professionally?

- How do you manage beginnings and endings?

- Do you think your own experience of dealing with transitions influences your practice?

- How can you practice stepping back from your own feelings about these issues and allowing yourself to view each child's unique needs in this area afresh?

Links to the EYFS

Positive Relationships

Principle: Children learn to be strong and independent from a base of loving and secure relationships with parents and/or a key person.

Commitments

Respecting each other

Every interaction is based on caring professional relationships and respectful acknowledgement of the feelings of children and families.

Parents as partners

Parents are children's first and enduring educators. When parents and practitioners work together in Early Years settings, the results have a positive impact on children's development and learning.

Supporting learning

Warm trusting relationships with knowledgeable adults support children's learning more effectively than any other amount of resources.

Key person

A key person has special responsibilities for working with a small number of children, giving them the reassurance to feel safe and cared for and building relationships with their parents.

From the EYFS Principles into Practice: Card 2.2 – Positive Relationships – Key Person

Effective practice

- Ensure that rotas are based on when a key person is available for each child.

- Provide a second key person for children so that when the main key person is away there is a familiar and trusted person who knows the child well.

- Plan time for each key person to work with parents so that they really know and understand the children in their key group.

- As children move groups or settings, help them to become familiar with the new key person.

Challenges and dilemmas

- Reassuring others that children will not become too dependent on the key person or find it difficult to adjust to being a member of a group.

- Meeting children's needs for a key person while being concerned for staff who may well feel over-attached to a child.

- Reassuring parents who may be concerned that children may be more attached to staff than to them.

- Supporting children's transitions within and beyond a setting, particularly as children reach four or five years.

Links to the Early Years National Strategy – Social and Emotional Aspects of Development (SEAD)

From SEAD Guidance for Practitioners Working in the EYFS

Positive Relationships 3.1a, p. 21

The parent's view

For a parent to leave their child with another adult can be difficult to do at first. Any parent will be concerned that they know their child better than anyone else. Parents might wonder if the practitioners will:

- understand their child's communication;

- notice if their child is unwell;

- share concerns with them in a caring and understanding way;

- tell them what happens to their child through the day, sharing joys as well as sadness;

- involve them in their child's life in the setting by:
  - talking to them about their child and what they do in the setting and at home;
  - giving them photographs of their child in action in the setting;
  - encouraging them to take part in activities with their child.

Positive Relationships 3.1b, p. 23

Learning points

- It is very important to ensure that consideration is given to the well-being of staff.

- Working with and caring for young children makes heavy emotional demands on staff and they sometimes need support themselves.

- Allocating a buddy or mentor for a new member of staff is a useful strategy.

Positive Relationships 3.2, pp. 29 and 30

Children learn about people, relationships and ways of being with each other from the adults around them – whether we like it or not, adults are always modelling social and emotional skills for the children by:

- how they speak to each other, to individual children and groups of children;

- the way they treat each other when things go wrong;

- their body language;

- their facial expression.

Learning about relationships and the skills we need to maintain positive relationships is something which happens all through our lives. In our work with young children it is important that we also learn things about ourselves; for example, how we deal with our emotions and how this has changed over time.

Reflect and note

- How you show you are happy, sad, angry, worried.

- Your own first sign you are feeling one of these emotions.

- Strategies which are effective for you to deal with your feelings. This will mean you can still be professional and supportive even when you feel one of these emotions.

- Which of these emotions would it help you to be able to deal with in a different way?

- What are you going to do about it?

Learning points

- Observation is the key to finding solutions for children who are struggling to manage their feelings.

- By observing closely, practitioners can find what happens before the child behaves in an anti-social way, exactly how they react and what happens now.

- Then practitioners can take appropriate action based on assessment of the child in the whole situation and plan for the best ways forward for all the children's personal, social and emotional development.

- Children's friendships are very important for their well-being. Children who find it difficult to be friendly are usually very unhappy and need sensitive and sustained support from practitioners.

Enabling environments

How the wider context and its living web
of relationships influences the core of
Early Years practice

A practitioner's account

Practitioners have an opportunity to participate in a shared observation of heuristic play.

A group of childcare practitioners are sitting quietly having watched a 20 minute film on 'heuristic play'. They have been able to observe a group of children from 12 to 20 months, discovering for themselves the pleasure of experimenting in an environment where there is no failure just uninterrupted exploration. Children have been using natural physical objects to rattle, roll, swing, tip, and pour. They have been doing this in close proximity to other children following their own journey of stacking, twisting, tapping, pulling and placing. There have been occasional cooperative moments of sharing, little whoops of pleasure and gasps of satisfaction from the children we watch. We have heard the murmur of a tune being sung and the momentarily attuned helping hand of an adult, who quietly blends back into the background. These children have been absorbed in the serious business of play and activity. They have been lost in thought and alive to the infinite possibilities of their exploring. This enabling environment has been facilitated by the adults who have arranged the room, attended and through their silent attuned presence have responded to every sound and movement of the play. They have fitted in with the child's experience, been emotionally available, and by so doing become the enabling environment and part of this atmosphere of discovery. There is nothing subdued in this calmness but a vibrant atmosphere of self-discovery and hopefulness. Not for the first time, following the watching of this film, I am struck by the thoughtful silence and invite these practitioners to share their thoughts.

Practitioners are often struck by the levels of concentration and calmness they have observed and they are curious about the role of the adults who have not interrupted the children's concentration by making endless verbal interactions. They wonder, too, about how they have created environments in their settings, where there seem to be so few opportunities for children to develop the 'capacity to be alone' in the presence of another (Winnicott 1958). There are immediate ideas about how it might be possible to:

- shape the culture in their settings;
- create calm periods in the day;
- re-look at how the physical space reflects and influences the emotional climate.

In my experience, practitioners' willingness to share their insights with each other in this way comes about when they are offered as adults a peaceful learning environment which enables them to think.

I have begun this chapter with an account of a group of practitioners responding to a setting other than their own. What this group have observed is a different environment, which has been created and maintained through specific attention to detail. They have been able to step back and look at the whole picture of the environment, the children and the adults, and with these three corners of the triangle established, witness the quality of learning and development that can take place within the space. The film has beautifully demonstrated an enabling environment where there is:

- a sense of well-being and security;
- harmony in the space created, which allows 'doing' and 'being';
- capable and competent learners;
- staff with a space to observe, think, reflect, rethink and learn.

Conducting the symphony of the setting

In this chapter, I am going to focus on the adults conducting the symphony of the setting. I imagine anyone who has facilitated the care and learning of a group of children will recognise it as being at times like making music. One is aware, on one hand when things feel 'out of tune' and when at other times activity flows. The conductor senses with every fibre of their being when free-flow play feels chaotic and frantic, and at other times when there is a rhythm, vitality and a sense of purposefulness, i.e. it really flows!

In this chapter we will take a step back and look at the emotional environment created by all the people who are a part of it and the thought that is given to primary care – beginnings, feeding, sleeping, resting, warmth and endings.

We observe children, like Ellie in Chapter 2 discovering new things for themselves when enabling environments are created and we have begun to think about whether this is true for staff too, who are offered spaces to think and feel. In other words, is there a parallel process for staff working in this field? I wish to propose that if we nurture the Early Years nurturers and offer spaces and frameworks to think, then there will be significant new discoveries about practice in relation to personal, social and emotional development for practitioners.

We can rearrange the furniture in the toddler room or hang a new mobile from the ceiling of our baby rooms but how do we rearrange our thinking in terms of creating enabling environments that allow for psychological holding and containment?. What do I mean by the terms 'holding' and 'containing'? We have been exploring throughout the book in different ways how mothers take in the emotional lives of babies and digest what they are offered. They then through attunement give back appropriate care to the baby and show by so doing, sensitive nurturing which communicates affection and love. The baby's pleasure in having their needs met is a mutually satisfying experience. However, mothers who are overwhelmed cannot provide this function very easily and leave the infant feeling helpless and overwhelmed too.

Practitioners who feel overwhelmed

So, what happens I wonder if a team of staff in a children's centre are like a struggling mother and are feeling overwhelmed by:

- difficult feelings relating to when a child requires extensive support for their feelings of sadness, anger or frustration (EYFS Principles into Practice: Card 3.3 – Enabling Environments – Reflecting on Practice, DfES 2007b)
- feelings of anxiety and uncertainty about the implementation of a new framework like the EYFS;
- feelings of fear about being scrutinised by Ofsted;

- unexpected sadness about their own early experiences of childhood 'woken up' in them by working closely with young children;

- insecurity about their place in the team and finding their voice with colleagues;

- the amount of paperwork they have to complete, which they feel creates a barrier to their relationships with children.

Just reading through this list helps us to imagine how your mind as a practitioner might become full up and preoccupied by the many aspects of your work environment. One of the areas often unattended to by staff is their sense of loss and sadness when they have to say goodbye to the young children who have been in their care and finding renewed energy to create new relationships. Sitting with a child who is crying can also stir feelings of personal loss and separation and teasing out what is the practitioner's experience and the what is the child's is essential to developing good professional practice.

> One helpful thing to remember when we have a distraught infant in our arms crying 'mummy, mummy!' is that we are not only experiencing his immediate distress but that his cries may well have touched off a resonance on our own past experience which makes the situation doubly upsetting.
> (Goldschmied and Jackson 1994: 52)

So, what enabling environments can we offer practitioners so they can have reflective spaces to explore their feelings and so become more available to the children in their care? I would suggest an important part of creating an enabling environment for staff will be to include:

- supervision;

- collaborative problem-solving and reflective practice staff groups;

- developing a culture of management that recognises the symbolic meaning of what happens in the environment.

What is supervision?

Supervision is an opportunity for each practitioner (supervisee) to bring their thoughts and feelings about their key group of children to an experienced professional colleague (supervisor) and for both parties to have a reflective conversation about chosen issues and situations.

Supervision can be a very important part of taking care of one's self, staying open to new learning: and an indispensible part of the helper's well being, on-going self-development, self-awareness and commitment to development. We think that lack of supervision can contribute to feelings of staleness, rigidity, and defensiveness.

(Hawkins and Shohet 2006)

Supervision for Early Years practitioners

It is important that staff have monthly supervision when they are working closely with children of this age who have strong emotional needs. Ideally, this should be conducted by someone with a sound knowledge of conducting individual supervision and/or facilitating work discussion groups. This might be:

- a line manager, who is the best person, as they have an understanding of the particular demands of the setting; or
- an external supervisor, who may provide a fresh set of eyes and ears.

Offering this facility to all staff emphasises that everyone is an integral part of creating the whole emotional environment. Key support staff like centre secretaries and the other office staff, as we have discussed, are central to building relationships with parents and should be offered supervision, too.

Supervision should be given a high priority in the staff timetable:

- It should take place at a regular time and in a regular place.
- If it has to be cancelled for any reason, a new date should be set immediately.

For practitioners, the process of supervision offers an opportunity to rely on a space where they can share the demands of being a key person and makes the possibility of meeting their key children's needs realisable. Staff can also share their disappointments, struggles, and inter-staff tensions. Over time it can become possible to develop one's own internal supervisor, which may mean that between supervision sessions you are able to name some of the feelings that are stirred up inside you. For example, it may be that you are 'losing' one of your babies to the toddler room and whilst approaching this preparation for the transition positively, you feel unexpectedly tearful and sad. When one has experienced an enabling environment like supervision over a considerable time, it can become possible to talk about one's attachments and feelings like this about separation and loss.

These feelings may be sometimes avoided or 'managed away' by many staff, which may be detrimental to the children in their care. There are plenty of ways of not developing close relationships with children, like using paperwork to build barriers and being very busy all the time as a safe way of not getting involved. These complex feelings require sensitive understanding. However, once in a safe professional supervisory relationship, one begins to recognise one's response to these events and how it may fit with one's own personal experiences of change. It can be a great relief to make these connections between the personal and professional and so disentangle feelings which can get in the way of our capacity to think through a situation and act in the best interests of the child.

It is also healthy to voice anxieties within the team, for it can often be what is *not* said that causes most damage, for teams cannot take responsibility for what is hidden. Voicing fears within the staff group can mirror helping children to develop their capacity for emotional literacy. The relief for the team as a whole, when one member of a team says: 'I'm really anxious about all these new health and safety directives and how they may take away all my spontaneity with the children. Does anyone else feel the same?' Now there is a possibility for the team to take shared responsibility for what may have been a silent anxiety for others as well.

How sharing can maximise Early Years practitioners' competence

Collaborative problem-solving groups

Collaborative problem-solving groups provide an opportunity to reflect with others on practice and find ways forward.

Do you remember Khalid at the beginning of this book? Well there are many children who to some degree are asking to be in practitioners' minds and it can be very helpful when a group of staff have an opportunity to explore together a specific child who is preoccupying a staff member and who wishes to deepen their understanding of the child. The work in this field of enquiry developed by Gerda Hanko (1999) to increase competence and problem-solve as a whole staff team is invaluable to Early Years staff.

By following a clear structure with time boundaries and offering a consultative approach, it can be possible to:

- see beyond the behaviour and gauge a child's needs;
- build on the many good aspects of a child or parent;
- explore in the supportive presence of colleagues new possibilities for working with children;
- restore confidence in individual staff members and the team as a whole.

How does this approach work?

- Establish confidentiality within the group.
- Invite a practitioner to present the salient features of their current difficulty.
- The group then asks clarifying questions (things they feel they would like a bit more detail about).
- The group then offers the presenting colleague through a 'wondering aloud' process their thoughts, using open questions in one of the following ways:
  - ○ What would happen if ...?
  - ○ Could it be that ...?
  - ○ Do you think ...?
  - ○ How would it feel if ...?
  - ○ How might this child/parent respond to ...?
- Finally, there is time for the presenting member of the group to give feedback on the process to the group and share some of how they might use what they have heard in the service of the child.

To give the reader a clearer idea of the quality thinking and shared knowledge that can follow this process, we will return to Khalid in Chapter 1, and discover the new thoughts given to Sally, his carer, following help from the team in the above way. A collaborative problem-solving group with the whole staff team contributed some of the following new thinking to the perceived difficulty:

- Staff realised they did not know what the thinking was behind Khalid attending two afternoons a week. Did Mum work or did she want to extend his socialisation? Was his attendance about early education?
- The staff did not know anything about the Islamic faith or cultural beliefs about weaning.

- Staff noticed there was a feeling of walking 'on egg shells' and a lack of curiosity about enquiring about some of these interesting areas of discovery.

- The staff wondered whether their own lack of curiosity has something to do with Khalid's inability to be curious and explore the play space.

- Staff were anxious about getting things wrong.

- Would it be possible to make a home visit to forge stronger home-setting links?

- Could it be that Khalid was not bonding with his key person because he was bonded to his mother through the breastfeeding?

- Could his mother bring expressed milk to the nursery for snack time?

- How might his mother respond to being asked to bring a comforter, like a scarf of hers to the nursery to help with the transition from home?

- What might happen if Khalid had a fresh start at nursery with his mother being involved in a planned separation rather than her continuing with her quick exits, which leave Khalid so distressed?

- What would happen if Mum was invited to join one of the walks to the duck pond so she could see it was a safe excursion?

- Would she enjoy taking part in a nursery activity?

- Could other family members be involved in bringing Khalid to nursery?

- The group wondered about making a little family book so that Khalid was comforted by looking at the photographs of his family and pets and offered gentle verbal reassurance at the times he was very unsettled.

- Staff wondered how children of Khalid's age conceived of time and felt it would be helpful for children to have a visual aid showing arriving and leaving with parents and what happened in between these times.

Suddenly, what were perceived as areas of difficulty, through an enabling and reflective professional environment opened up as new avenues of possible exploration and fresh understanding.

The enabling environment as a metaphor for maternal care

Most Early Years practitioners will spend a considerable time first thing in the morning preparing their rooms for the arrival of their group of babies or children. This will include attending to lighting, the temperature and ventilation of the room. Meanwhile, staff in the reception area are receiving early morning phone calls and preparing to greet parents upon their arrival. The day's communication network has begun long before the children arrive. At one level these are daily tasks but they also have symbolic meaning and communicate a series of important messages. Children not only respond to what is said to them and the tone of voice we use but they have a 'nose for the smell of a place'. So for example, a child who is used to calm, security and warmth will have a nose for a rushed atmosphere and any chilly winds between staff. Equally, a child who has known domestic violence will have a radar-like accuracy for sensing the hierarchy of a setting and where the authority structures are and how they are used. Other children, who have experienced parental depression, will know when morale is low or when the staff are preoccupied with other things and so are unable to hold them in their minds.

Attention should also be given to the spiritual environment of a setting which strengthens and is a source of resilience. Seemingly small details of care are etched into our memory and experience and nourish us in invisible ways. Attending to the things around us and becoming sensitive to details like fresh flowers, careful routines and the expressions on our faces is a way of helping children to discover the joy of life and being part of a community.

Figure 5.1 Learning through purposeful activity and exploration

The entrance to the setting

What does the entrance/threshold to your setting say about what you stand for and value as a staff group? Why do I highlight this part of the environment when there is so much of interest going on inside the setting? For arguments sake, I shall be very literal for a moment and then look at the more subtle meaning of what we convey about ourselves through the environment. If, let us say, there was a fireplace in the entrance hallway to your nursery, as there once might have been years ago, and on a winter's morning it was lit, what would we be saying to those who cross the threshold, beyond heating the area?

- There is a heart to this community.
- You are expected and we have spent time preparing for you.
- You can expect warmth and care here.

Well there are not many open fires in nurseries today but an arrangement of fresh flowers in the porch offers a message about beauty and care, and plants say something about aliveness and growth. A Treasure Basket full of conkers in the autumn and shells and pebbles in the summer inside the front door is an act of care, the underlying message of which matters.

Are parents immediately confronted by blown-up EYFS practice cards on the wall as they enter or are there examples of children's artwork in view? What difference does it make if the latter is in the background and the EYFS is in the foreground? What message do you want to convey to children about the ingredients of the setting by making one or other choice?

Food as an expression of love and care

Likewise, is lunchtime a timetabled event to be got through and cleared away as quickly as possible or do we wish to convey a message in the detail and thought given to this primary care context? Is there a tablecloth and a bowl of fresh fruit on the table? How appealing are the place settings? Have children designed their own place mats? After all, food can be something that arrives at a set time each day or it can be valued at a deeper level as being about sharing, belonging, providing a sense of well-being and comfort within a communal setting. If we are in agreement that it is so, then we are brought back full circle to attachment, because food is an expression of a carer's attachment to her babies and children and a fundamental function of any loving and caring relationship.

Could we use our observational skills to create an enabling environment that believes that these acts of thoughtfulness matter and have a powerful impact on both those who have produced them and those in receipt of such gifts? A relaxed setting facilitates these times of close physical proximity, warmth and intimacy and the family atmosphere, which helps children to feel an adult's intuitive capacity to nurture. Recently a group of practitioners were describing how they balanced sheets on their knees and ticked boxes relating to what each individual child at the table ate. The task of recording this information was the priority in this setting and the process of eating was given little symbolic importance. It is important to ask yourselves whether these things really matter.

Food as a symbol of maternal care in reception classes

The challenge of preserving calm spaces across the day may be keenly felt by reception class teachers who exist within busy educational settings and where there may be an emphasis upon content of the curriculum rather than process. However, the EYFS is offering an opportunity to extend the key person approach and Early Years practice into reception classes and in cooperation with colleagues in nurseries and children's centres to share good practice. As we discussed in the previous chapter, this will help make the transition to school seamless and present children with an extension of the community they knew and the new community they are joining.

So, in reception classes it can be very comforting for children to enjoy their food in familiar surroundings rather than marching across each day to the big, echoing school canteen with the clatter of trays and cutlery. Reception class teachers may wish to keep this daily sharing as a small group experience for the first half-term and keep a safe boundary around it for their new reception class children. Some of the older children might like to visit and join the reception children as lunch guests in their classroom. This preparation for eventual transition to the dining room will mean the familiar faces of the lunch guests will eventually sit at their tables and be known to them.

Nurturing good enough relationships with staff

Finally, managers can become an important connection with the enabling environment by being open and available to staff and actively engaged in hearing any underlying concerns within the team. At times of change this may just involve listening to adult anxieties with a spirit of quiet acceptance. Belief that attending to the environment in the thoughtful ways suggested as above, will then spread through the setting in many new and exciting ways and pass into the culture or ethos as if by osmosis. Nurturing good enough staff relationships and connecting with staff is the foundation upon which sensitive work with children is built. As a manager working together with staff so they see how you are with parents and children and what you do in any given situation is worth any number of training days! Of course, it is very important that managers offering supervision have regular supervision themselves. Practitioners are desperate to work in an environment which enables them to be realistic about what is manageable and we all seek continuity in care in our work contexts in order to thrive professionally.

Learning about the wider community

No setting is hermetically sealed from the outside world. If we are social beings from the beginning and dependent on others and each other then what is happening in the wider world will have a direct impact on children. Therefore it should be remembered that although nursery staff are attempting to create a benign and safe environment for all children, an awareness of the external realities for many children has meant they have been directly affected by poverty, recession and parental distress.

They will benefit from knowing and experiencing the spaces directly surrounding the buildings and the wider community of which they are a part. Visits to local amenities and invitations to people who work and live in the immediate community help children to expand their horizons and gain a sense of their place in the world which goes beyond the four walls of the nursery. Nursery schools that have existed for years on the same site have a history which can be represented through photographic memories and so a sense of past, present and future is conceived in a tangible way.

We have talked about the mother mirroring the baby's experience and it is equally important for a 'large mirror', so to speak, to be held up to the wider context of family and culture, which is after all part of children's existing experience and identity. Continuing to develop a sense of place by exploring the outside world beyond the immediate outside areas of the setting is about knowing one's roots in a community and striding out, running and touching the political, social, religious and cultural world as a citizen. These ideas of attachment to a place and culture pose real challenges for staff who find themselves on sites close to motorway slip roads, in industrial estates or positioned in the corner of a supermarket site and raise important questions to planners about freedom of access to local facilities for children beyond a view of the busy commercial world alone.

How to make a positive contribution to good practice

- Managers should attune to staff's non-verbal cues when they are gathered as a team, e.g. being late for team meetings on a regular basis, the tone of conversations when staff are having their breaks, the kind of humour there is in the setting. These may be signs of difficulties being avoided or not being talked about openly.

- Wondering aloud about what might be happening when you are not certain can lead to others sharing responsibility collectively for what is happening in a team.

- Make it a priority that you revisit regularly the wider context and consider what it feels like not only for staff, parents and children to enter your nursery but for other outside professionals visiting.

- Asking for help with supporting an enabling context will demonstrate that asking for help in general is a strength not a weakness.

- Managers, who delegate and let go of certain administrative tasks, have time to spend at grass roots level experiencing the daily challenges of the staff.

- Make sure significant events in staff lives are remembered, e.g. birthdays, anniversaries of losses, and demonstrate in your management style a basic principle of attachment thinking so that staff expectations of being met as people are fulfilled.

- The case studies and learning points in the National Strategy – Social and Emotional Aspects of Development (SEAD) provide an excellent resource to develop induction programmes for new staff , to use in staff development and team-building sessions within the setting.

Your personal reflections

- Bring to mind an occasion recently when you felt you connected well with people at work.
- Are there times when this does not happen?
- Can you think about what it was that made a difference to these two experiences?
- What could you do more of to enable yourself to thrive at work and make good professional attachment relationships?

Links to the EYFS

Enabling Environments

Principle: The environment plays a key role in supporting and extending children's development.

Commitments

Observation, assessment and planning

Babies and young children are individuals first, each with a unique profile of abilities. Schedules and routines should flow with the child's needs. All planning starts with observing children in order to understand and consider their current interests, development and learning.

Supporting every child

The environment supports every child's learning through planned experiences and activities that are challenging and achievable.

The learning environment

A rich and varied environment supports children's learning and development. It gives them the confidence to explore and learn in secure and safe, yet challenging, indoor and outdoor spaces.

The wider context

Working in partnership with other settings, other professionals and with individuals and groups in the community supports children's development and progress towards the outcomes of Every Child Matters; being healthy, staying safe, enjoying and achieving, making a positive contribution, and economic well-being.

From the EYFS Principles into Practice: Card 3.3 – Enabling Environments – The Learning Environment

The emotional environment

- The emotional environment is created by all the people in the setting, but adults have to ensure that it is warm and accepting of everyone.

- Adults need to empathise with children and support their emotions.

- When children feel confident in the environment they are willing to try things out, knowing that effort is valued.

- When children know that their feelings are accepted they learn to express them, confident that the adults will help them with how they are feeling.

Reflecting on practice

- What support is available to practitioners who may feel 'drained' emotionally when a child requires extensive support for their feelings of sadness, anger or frustration?

From the EYFS Principles into Practice: Card 3.4 – Enabling Environments – The Wider Context

Effective practice

- Ensure that parents are kept informed in advance about what will happen at transition times, such as when children join the setting.

- Involve parents at transition times, valuing what they say and encouraging them to stay with their children while they settle in.

- When children attend several settings ensure the practitioners from each setting regularly share the children's development and learning records and any other relevant information.

- Take time to listen to colleagues from other professional backgrounds and be open about differences of language and approach.

Challenges and dilemmas

- Finding time to record children's progress and development in ways which can be easily shared across agencies.

- Finding sufficient time to really involve parents fully in decisions made about their children.

- Maintaining good relationships with professionals whom you only see once in a while.

Links to the Early Years National Strategy – Social and Emotional Aspects of Development (SEAD)

From SEAD Guidance for Practitioners Working in the EYFS

Enabling Environments 4.1, p. 34

Learning points

- The most important resource in any Early Years setting are the practitioners who work there. They have to mediate images and resources.

- When new resources are introduced it is important to talk with children about them, to model ways of using them and to connect them with children's lives and experience and let the children air their views and questions.

- In this way children's knowledge and understanding of the wider community they are part of – a key aspect of social development – is fostered.

- Children are less likely to behave hurtfully to others who are different from them if they encouraged to see each other as special and unique and to understand the things that make them similar and different from each other. This contributes to children developing the skills of empathy with others.

Enabling Environments 4.2, pp. 35 and 36

Reflect and note

- How do you as a staff team respond if and when young children make discriminatory comments about differences?

- The time that you spend discussing and reflecting on your own attitudes and practice – or do you avoid doing it because it may be uncomfortable?

- What is it like for different children and families in your setting?

- How do you enable children to take sensible risks? If we never learn what it is like to have a scraped knee or a bruised elbow – to feel the pain and know it passes – we will probably be very nervous about challenging ourselves in new situations.

NB. See Appendix 2: Reflections on the emotionally enabling environment, in SEAD Practitioners' Guide (DCSF 2008: 53). This is an audit for use with parents, practitioners, leaders and children. The purpose of which is to support staff teams in making a judgement about how they look after and promote personal, social and emotionally well-being for everyone in the setting, not just the children.

CHAPTER 6

Learning and development

Attachment, emotional growth and learning

A practitioner's account

Practitioners have a direct experience of play at a workshop.

A group of Early Years practitioners are using a variety of art materials to explore the theme 'Play and me' for 15 minutes as part of a Treasure Basket workshop. There has been some nervous laughter because they say this is not something they usually do themselves despite supporting children in their play daily. The facilitator reassures them that there will be no 'show and tell' session at the end, and there is visible relief in the room as they all settle down to learn from this experience and develop their ideas in whatever direction they wish. As the session draws to a close there are smiles and one or two spontaneously wonder if they could show their creations to the group and talk about the process of playing. What learning and development has occurred in this peaceful oasis of time for these practitioners? Some of the group say how surprised they were by how anxious they felt initially. Others felt excited and derived so much pleasure from experimenting with the materials that they wondered why they did not do it more regularly. Someone says how rare it is to take part in a spontaneous self-chosen activity. One practitioner says she felt she was able to really enjoy the activity once she knew it would not be assessed by others and that she had a choice to show her work or not. The facilitator guides the discussion towards how successfully staff would be able to record what they have just experienced. How they would capture in words their own process of playing. Although everyday these Early Years staff are observing and recording learning and development, capturing their own meaningful narrative of their play is challenging. They reflect on their learning from experience that morning, and explore the value of checklists as a means of recording learning and development compared with a learning journey as part of an in-depth assessment tool. Each in different ways seems to have found it useful to remember their own emotional responses at the point of being invited 'just to play' and as a result are mindful of the obstacles to the learning process for many children. At the end of the day two group members ask if they can take their creations home.

Interestingly, the majority of practitioners who attend my workshops were brought up at home by a primary carer and started school aged 5 years old. Therefore, their early play experiences would not have been in large groups. The way in which children are being brought up is changing and it is worth spending time reflecting on the differences in early experiences and the changes currently occurring at an earlier age. Young children, who enter day childcare for long periods of time, are being required to adapt much sooner to a range of complex interactions, e.g.:

- becoming a group member;
- negotiating the complexity of a wide network of relationships;
- potential feelings of competitiveness in relation to others;
- potential experiences of failure compared to others and so feelings of shame.

Knowledge from an attachment perspective informs much of our thinking about the social and emotional aspects of learning and encourages us to look beyond being led by a structured curriculum but rather offering children dynamic learning activities which continue to strengthen healthy growth and development. The Early Years practitioner will be familiar with how personal, social and emotional development within the framework of the EYFS encourages them to attend to the unique child, create positive relationships and actively support through thoughtfulness, an enabling environment that acknowledges that children develop and learn in different ways and at different rates.

The EYFS as a tent

If we imagine the outer structure of the EYFS as being like a tent, then we know the value of checking the guy ropes, adjusting them properly so there is maximum space inside, with no sagging sides, thus offering security against the changing weather!

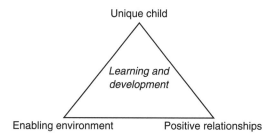

Figure 6.1 The EYFS 'tent'

If the tent of the EYFS is sound, then a space is created within it, where learning and development can flourish.

My experience of working with children who have been excluded from mainstream school has led me to believe that they have needed one or all of these guy ropes tightening before any learning can begin. One's capacity to engage in learning and develop involves being valued as a human being, trusting others in their willingness to make a relationship with you, and being surrounded by an environment that will support each individual through their unique learning journey and protect them from shame associated with failure.

In this chapter I want to make a connection between secure attachments and learning and how to recognise when young children are finding it a struggle to become curious, or develop through exploration and so learn. I hope that you are getting a sense from the previous chapters that if we take care of the baby/child, by taking care of relationships and actively caring for the environment of the setting, then we will be naturally attending to children's emotional states. This allows children in turn to enjoy activity, develop autonomy and a disposition to be curious, explore safely and learn with high levels of interest and cognition. The emphasis on the personal, social and emotional aspects of learning leads us to identify how affect comes first followed by cognition.

We have learned that enjoying a task for its own sake or being able to play freely and happily can be for some children as challenging as forming a relationship. In fact, we might even say that a child's capacity to make a relationship with the world through objects, new situations and free play is dependent on their experience of previous relationships. The securely attached child has a sense of well-being, trusts others enough to believe the world in general is safe and does not fear failing but views every new challenge as a learning journey.

Understandably, when a child's engagement with the world does not flow and there is not an innate sense of pleasure for the child in their achievements, practitioners are puzzled and concerned. When staff are working together in a collaborative problem solving group (see Chapter 5) and reflecting on their practice there are common preoccupations for staff about certain children.

What concerns practitioners

- He does not seem to be able to settle to anything for long.
- She cannot get started on her own.
- His concentration is very poor.
- She plays alone and never interacts with others.
- I feel like I am being kept at arm's length.
- He is 4 years old and everything still goes into his mouth.
- She cannot share or cooperate when learning in a small group.
- He gives up easily and is reluctant to have another go.
- She does not speak or express anything about what she is doing or experiencing.
- He follows me around and cannot play unless I am by his side.

Geddes (2006) in her book *Attachment in the Classroom* suggests there may be a link between a child's attachment style and their capacity to attach to tasks, ask for help and overcome difficulties when learning. This text is invaluable to reception class teachers and may inform Early Years practitioners' observation skills relating to learning and development.

If we think about children who have experienced unpredictable parenting and who therefore find it difficult to be explorers and curious learners, we begin to understand the role of the secondary attachment figure as an attuned presence helping children to:

- trust that learning is a dialogue;
- feel safe enough to be fully absorbed in play;
- develop a sense of predictability about the learning environment;
- trust that adults will be sensitive to their needs.

So how can practitioners make a difference to children who struggle to enjoy play spontaneously?

They can do this by:

- being a calm reassuring presence with children who are anxious;

- preparing children for any change of routine: 'In five minutes … when the hand on the clock … we are going to';

- offering enough emotional scaffolding to help the child fasten on to an activity and then briefly withdrawing but returning at intervals;

- communicating with non-verbal signals that you are close by, available if needed and that an activity can offer safety and enjoyment;

- being an unobtrusive yet attuned and reliable presence during activities such as Treasure Basket and heuristic play;

- being aware of 'how near – how far' in relation to the amount of space between yourself and the child;

- asking children if it is alright to sit by them and watch their play;

- offering gentle commentaries on the play of children who find it hard to be 'in relationship' with others: 'I can see you are burying the farmer in the sand and now you have uncovered him and he is standing up and is on his way again … .'

- showing the play experiences on offer, but not allowing the child to feel pressurised to participate (Hughes 2006);

- experiencing the benefit of supportive, positive and open communication between the parent and the caregiver (Hughes 2006).

The world of play

When we observe secure children playing we are aware from an attachment perspective that, although they may have entered a personal universe in their total absorption, they are doing so within the enabling climate provided by a secure adult presence. Whether this is a primary caregiver or a secondary attachment figure the adult presence should be attentive and responsive but not intrusive. By attuning to a child's experience in this way, the carer becomes the atmosphere of it. Developing the capacity to be alone in the presence of another for very young children does not require any 'doing' from the carer who is present. It is in the atmosphere of attunement and 'being' that the child speaks for himself, just as later in adulthood we speak within ourselves.

Figure 6.2 An adult facilitates learning and development in a small group

Assisting development and learning – 'doing' or 'being' as a practitioner?

I wish to highlight aspects of two Early Years activities that demonstrate the role of the practitioner as an attuned adult facilitating learning and development: Treasure Basket and Heuristic Play. For when the principles laid down for this practice are adhered to as intended by Elinor Goldschmied (1994), and more recently by Anita Hughes (2006), then we have a model for the promotion of learning and development which can become a transferable skill. *Developing Play for the Under 3s – The Treasure Basket and Heuristic Play* by Anita Hughes (2006) is the richest and most accessible text describing in depth and insightfully the process of open- ended purposeful play.

In brief, and in order to offer examples of how learning and development can unfold in deceptively simple ways, I shall summarise the process and highlight the pivotal role of adults in their function of 'being' rather than 'doing'.

Treasure Basket 'is where an adult offers a seated baby (who cannot yet move independently) a range of natural, household and recycled objects, contained in a rigid low-sided round basket, for exploration and interest. It is a deceptively simple idea but these objects form the initial gateway towards independent contact with the outside world and create the first opportunity for making choices and decisions. This is the developmental stage in infancy where the predominant interest is to handle and mouth objects in order to find out about their physical characteristics. If a baby had language his main questions would be: "What is this object like?"' (Hughes 2006).

Heuristic play or 'discovery' play is experimental play, prepared by an adult who provides a range of natural materials and objects and then commences a journey of scientific discovery that centres around: 'What else can I do with this?'

Both of these events are presented in a boundaried, calm setting and are 'non-social' activities that promote concentration. The objects are laid out in advance of the session, at the end of the session there is a calm clearing up in which the children participate naturally, for it is an extension of the activity of sorting and placing objects in their 'correct' place. What is worth thinking about is how little direct intervention there is from another, unless an adult makes a thoughtful intervention to assist an object that rolls out of sight with Treasure Basket time, or offers another object when two children want the same object or when a child has set themselves an impossible task, e.g. pushing a ball which is too large down a tube.

How do we facilitate this kind of learning confidently? By trusting the process and inherent curiosity of children and letting them 'be'. It might be that if an Ofsted inspector were to enter into a Treasure Basket or heuristic play session, there might be some real curiosity about what was happening and most importantly what exactly the practitioner's role was, for it might appear as though they were doing nothing of any value. Responding confidently to such interest requires understanding the difference between content and process.

Process: what is your role as a practitioner during heuristic play?

Attunement during this discovery play involves:

- trusting that innumerable, low key, small non-verbal actions have a greater impact than previously thought on the developing mind of the child in terms of shaping the world they come to know;

- seeing observation as an opportunity to get to know individual children's differences, needs, interests and potential avenues of exploration *not* just as a tick-box task;

- being 'active' in your mind when observing and continuing to think beyond a recorded observation, and being alive to play activities as they continually change and unfold;

- remembering that a calm presence is a powerful intervention in itself;

- modelling non-verbal communication as a fundamental communication skill for understanding human interaction;

- knowing that picking up non-verbal cues plays a continuing part in a child's ability to learn and socialise;

- trusting, as an attuned mother with a very young baby does, that communication can be pre-verbal;

- knowing there is no single goal of development, that children do not think in isolation and that they learn through play, which is always changing.

Content: what are children learning?

They are learning to:

- discover through their senses;
- learn in a group;
- find joy and pleasure in their exploration;
- follow their instincts;
- explore cause and effect;
- make deep attachments to objects;
- observe, question, hypothesise and take risks;
- value feelings of trust and security.

Facilitating learning in different contexts

- Let children know what is happening whether it is at the whole group level, in a small group or with an individual child.

- Create a space within the physical setting for activity and play to take place.

- Walk around the setting regularly to get a sense of the physical space and how it helps or hinders learning and involve children and adults in adapting the setting.

- Manage the start and finish of a learning activity – even 'free flow' and open-ended activities begin and end!

- Be certain of the intention of an intervention. Is it to clarify, connect, explain, lead, link, model, support or summarise and so on?

- Make thoughtful verbal interventions. Is your comment or question intended to draw out a thought, feeling or sensation?

Recording children's learning and development

In the final part of this chapter, I am going to offer some thoughts about how to connect experiences of attachment to our recording and observing skills. When we are reviewing learning and development it is important that we record what we see in a way that has meaning for the child, parent and practitioner. It can be helpful to think of all documentation of this nature as a communication.

In order for our record keeping to reflect the whole picture of every child and to be true and committed to translating principles into practice, it is important to find a way of documenting learning and development. What exactly are you curious about? What surprised you as you observed a child?

Think about the current methods and tools you use for:

- recording

- identifying strengths and weaknesses

- assessing

- planning ahead.

Now ask yourself:

- Are you merely carrying out a task and if so what picture of the child are you achieving?

- Have you noticed whether you build up a more rounded picture by observing and listening over a longer period of time?

- If you are using a tick-box record sheet does this serve its purpose?

- Would your document of learning engage and interest parents and children?

- Do you record the child's experience of learning?
- Do you make a note of what has been unexpected for you as an observer?
- Is your account clear and useful?
- Do you share your observations regularly in full with colleagues?

There are increasing concerns about how we record and handle material relating to children in many spheres. The time spent filling out forms, or entering information on to computer systems, has replaced writing case notes in a narrative form. I wonder which format helps other professionals pick up more easily the details of a complex case. Certainly tick-box schedules can be a helpful guide for recording certain information but inevitably represent a partial view and lack precision in terms of identifying wider contextual influences on the child. There is a sense too that the current amounts of paperwork generated may be producing mountains so high that we cannot see each other over the summit of it! As practitioners it is important to assess whether at times the completion of paperwork becomes a convenient place to hide and a potential barrier to effective communication. Offering parents and children the opportunity to contribute to adapting existing material so as to meet the needs of children as individuals.

The Primary National Strategy – Creating the Picture (DfES 2007c) highlights the six principles of record keeping which are evident in good and effective practice in Early Years settings:

1. Record keeping must be meaningful and have purpose.
2. The task of keeping records must be manageable and sustainable.
3. Records must capture the range of children's attainment, achievement and progress.
4. Records will reflect the individuality of every child and the diversity of their backgrounds.
5. All significant participants in children's development and learning should contribute to information gathering.
6. Records should be shared with the child.

Learning stories

The work of Margaret Carr, in *Assessment in Early Childhood Settings* (2001) sheds much light in this area and her research favours learning dispositions and the narrative story as a framework for learning about children's learning. Let us see how her approach helps assess complex and ambitious outcomes rather than simple and low-level outcomes and goals. Her framework is clearly rooted in the importance of reciprocal relationships and group dynamics and is underpinned by emphasising emotional growth and learning. Her research has led to a model of recording observations that looks at the learner in action.

The practitioner writes an account of what they have observed – *the learning story* – which is an account of an interaction between a practitioner and child, between peers, or whilst being involved in an activity. A learning story might include the child's voice or the parent's voice in relation to learning and development.

There is often a photograph or series of photographs depicting the leaning process, bringing the account into focus visually for the reader.

The observer then draws out different ways in which the learner was 'ready, willing and able to participate' in the learning process, revealing a 'combination of inclination, sensitivity to occasion and the relevant skill and knowledge' (M. Carr 2001).

Each child's achievements are then documented as five domains of learning dispositions or decision points in learning stories:

1. taking an interest;

2. being involved;

3. persisting with challenge and persisting with difficulty and uncertainty;

4. expressing an idea, feeling and point of view;

5. taking responsibility, taking another point of view.

(Carr 2001)

It would be possible to link these learning dispositions to strands in the EYFS framework and, by recording the child or parent's voice, this form of assessment becomes a living record.

We might even consider whether we might also be able to make a correlation between the five domains of learning dispositions (above) and mapping attachment dispositions, e.g.:

1. secure enough to be ready, willing and able to learn;

2. finding pleasure in being absorbed and enjoying exploration with no sense of failure;

3. demonstrating resilience, by being able to bounce back;

4. being confident enough in the relationship to trust sharing a thought;

5. moving from dependency to independence.

There is considerable emphasis in the public sector upon assessing outcomes for children. However, if we incorporate into this approach the fact that people are continually changing in unique ways, in their own time and according to their previous experiences of unmet basic needs, then the depth and breadth of the learning journey format seems to offer an authentic tool for recording social, emotional and cognitive development.

How to make a positive contribution to good practice

- Create observational tools which reflect the fact that children do not follow the same route when it comes to learning and development.

- Always make space for parent's observations in your record keeping.

- Do your observations include reference to things that are hard to pin down, including the quality of the teaching–learning relationship?

- Think about how successful learning relationships can be carried across to new contexts when planning transitions.

- Make discussion an important part of any assessment process and include children in it.

- Make wall displays of the learning stories so they become living entities and are open for dialogue between staff, children and parents and not hidden inside folders.

Your personal reflections

- How do you feel on your way to a new training session?
- How do you respond to learning in a group situation?

- What memories from your education do you have of learning in close proximity to other learners?
- Can you remember past emotional experiences of being both successful and failing in a learning situation?

Links to the EYFS

Learning and Development

Principle: Children develop and learn in unique and different ways and at different rates and all areas of Learning and Development are equally important and interconnected.

Commitments

Children's play reflects their wide ranging interests and preoccupations. In their play children learn at their highest level. Play with peers is important for children's development.

Children learn best through physical and mental challenges. Active learning involves other peoples, objects, ideas and events that engage and involve children for sustained periods.

When children have opportunities to play with ideas in different ways and with a variety of resources, they discover connections and come to new and better understandings and ways of doing things. Adult support in this process enhances their ability to think critically and ask questions.

The EYFS is made up of six areas of learning and development. All areas of learning and development are connected to one another and are equally important. All areas of learning and development are underpinned by the Principles of the EYFS.

From the EYFS Principles into Practice: Card 4.2 – Learning and Development – Active Learning

Effective practice

- Ensure children's well-being and involvement in learning by making each child feel secure and confident, and allowing them some control over their learning.

- Have realistic expectations of every child based on information from parents, what children themselves 'tell' you and from observation.

- Review your environment to ensure that it is interesting, attractive and accessible to every child so that they can learn independently.

- Make learning plans for each child based on information gained from talking to them, their parents and your colleagues and by observing the child.

- Recognise that every child's learning journey is unique to them.

Challenges and dilemmas

- Making sufficient time for busy staff to reflect on what has been observed about individual children and to reach conclusions about what has been learned.

- How to make the principle of active learning a foundation for learning while maintaining a focus on planning for the group.

- Gradually giving children greater independence in their learning while retaining control over the curriculum.

- Giving children a particular line of enquiry given the constraints of your routines and access areas such as outdoor spaces.

Links to the Early Years National Strategy – Social and Emotional Aspects of Development (SEAD)

From SEAD Guidance for Practitioners Working in the EYFS

Learning and Development 5.2, p. 43

Provide experiences that help children to develop autonomy and a disposition to learn

Children therefore need:

- opportunities to share ideas through interaction;

- opportunities to use conversation to express their ideas, their thinking and their joy;

- an atmosphere offering warmth, humour and nurturing which values children's ideas and learning;

- interaction with adults who have high but realistic expectations of children;

- environments which allow freedom in the use of materials and space unrestricted by convention, allowing children's imagination to take precedence;

- encouragement to play and experiment with all aspects of the learning environment, with words, activities, song and movement;

- time to learn at their pace.

Give support and a structured approach to vulnerable children, 5.3, p. 44

Reflect and note

- How to ensure that you are aware of the personal, social and emotional development needs of all the children in your care.

- How quiet or reserved children are listened to as well as those who are boisterous and forthcoming.

- How to let children's play flow, and wait to be invited to be part of the game, rather than taking over.

All the principles underpinned in the Early Years Foundation Stage (EYFS) and the National Strategy – Early Years: Social and Emotional Aspects of Development (SEAD) can be developed at a whole school level from the Foundation Stage onwards through the curriculum resource: National Strategies – Primary – Social and Emotional Aspects of Learning (SEAL). This material focuses on five social and emotional aspects of learning; self-awareness, managing feelings, motivation, empathy and social skills.

CHAPTER 7

Endings

Arriving back where we began

A practitioner's account

A practitioner's encounter with the dynamics of attachment in a wider setting.

Becoming more aware of the patterns of attachment

I am standing in a primary school playground. The new reception class children are in their own special outdoor area, marked by a bench beyond which the older children play with a free-wheeling, whirl of activity. A few children sit on the boundary bench watching the younger children and then occasionally turning to the squeals of their peers, joining in and then returning to the bench again.

In the reception class play area, two adults attend to clusters of children coming and going. One or two children stay very close to the adult, hold their hands tightly, needing to stay right by their side. Others journey back and forth showing things they have picked up, checking back with the huddle around the adult, listening in briefly to any conversation going on, and then are off again. Some children play alone as far away as possible from the hub of activity and enjoy finding places to hide away. Another small group are involved in imaginative group play. The adults stand out like markers on the horizon, steam rising from the cups of tea that have just arrived for them on this cold morning. This whole scene of movement reminds us of how in a familiar environment it is possible to lose oneself in walking, running, talking, singing, picking up a leaf, throwing a stone, searching for an insect amid the wood pile, but at any moment which feels a bit strange, we seek connectedness with another in order for our feelings to be organised. If we have not had this experience of an attuned response, we develop strategies to cope alone. Moment to moment this playground scene of children in brightly coloured coats, hats and gloves is like a kaleidoscope which changes according to what triggers the dynamics of attachment.

The EYFS urges practitioners to look, listen and note. The above scene is an example of the many environments in which it is possible to be naturally curious as a practitioner and to learn from the group as a whole.

Circle of Security

In this final chapter I am going to return to what we have learned from attachment thinking about what infants and small children really need. There is a wonderful piece of work from the USA called 'Circle of Security' (Cooper *et al.* 1998) which helps vulnerable parents understand about their unpredictable responses to their children. Some parents have a limited knowledge of attunement due to their own deprivations during their upbringing. They may experience their children's requests for care as overwhelming, persecuting or unbearable and by entering into a group programme they are able to observe through discussion and observing themselves on video how learning about attuning improves their child–parent relationships. The outcomes are very moving, as the caregiving systems in the parents participating in the programme are woken up and their children's needs begin to be understood and met.

The group programme includes the use of a visual aid to help parents understand the key to meeting a child's need for safety and security. The Circle of Security graphic is a rich and helpful summary of the key points of this book and the diagram below is a possible map you can carry in your mind in order to orientate yourself in your caregiving capacities.

Whether you are with a group of young children observing outdoor play or sitting across the table from a child picking up a paintbrush and painting a picture for the first time, the Circle of Security demonstrates so beautifully the atmosphere of careseeking and caregiving:

- Young children only develop within relationships and not alone or on their own.
- Adults who miss children's cues leave them emotionally unprotected.
- Young children who have early experiences of rejection expect to be rejected and so go on to reject others.
- An empathic response acknowledging a child's fears helps children process uncertainty and calms them.
- Remaining with the child's experience requires the adult to be 'bigger, stronger, wiser and kinder' (Cooper *et al.* 1998).

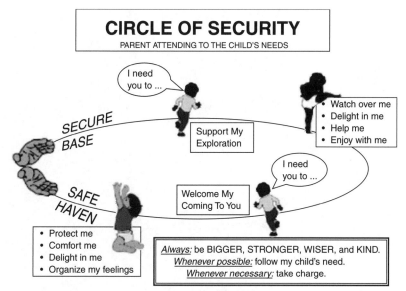

Figure 7.1 Travelling around the Circle of Security

Source: © 1998 Cooper, Hoffman, Marvin and Powell

It might be helpful to think about 'placing' your parents on the Circle of Security. For parents too may require their attachment needs attended to at points of separation and transition, having left their children with secondary caregivers. Practitioners may have a role to play in delighting in parents, supporting and organising their feelings and welcoming them back at the end of each day.

The application of this sensitivity to parental needs and the care given to routine encounters at the doorway of your setting are significant communications in terms of the success you will have in building trust and rapport. How we conduct ourselves as practitioners in our meetings and greetings, consultations and parent meetings really matters.

Una McCluskey in her book *To Be Met as a Person* explores how professionals can meet the needs of others seeking care. Raising our awareness of our responsiveness and sensitivity during these encounters seems to have direct relevance to Early Years practitioners, during what might otherwise be dismissed as insignificant everyday exchanges.

> It seems to me that careseekers read our faces and respond to what they see there, just as we read other's faces and respond to their expressions. Reading faces is where emotional arousal and the need for emotional regulation begins (and began in the past). Not having one's face read accurately and responded to empathically is clearly where a lot of pre-verbal pain is located.
>
> (McCluskey 2005)

Figure 7.2 Spontaneous mirroring between a child and practitioner

Some of the more difficult relationships that can develop with parents, when practitioners feel drawn to some parents more others and those who become perceived by staff as awkward, may have their roots in practitioners missing parental cues.

Being delighted in

Everybody entering an Early Years setting needs to feel it is a place that will receive them, and value and nurture their unique contribution. There is a very specific way in which professional colleagues mirror this capacity; by being able to stand in their colleague's shoes in their various roles and being curious and empathic in relation to each other. We can do this in small ways knowing that there is a significant impact on our relationships with colleagues when we extend our caregiving gifts to those seeking care.

The emotional climate

Are you able to remember your initial impressions of your setting when you attended for interview? What drew you to wanting to work there? Are you curious to remember what it feels like to start on your first day in a nursery when you are newly qualified? Do you have the capacity to wonder what it is like returning to work after a day at college? Do you wonder what your colleague learned at college yesterday? Are you interested or resentful that you had more to do in her absence? Do you wonder what it feels like to be your manager and to have the responsibility for the whole context? Empathic responsiveness between adults is part of the enabling environment.

Adults who are attuned to babies and young children offer a secure base: an emotional safe haven. Practitioners who enter the dance by being on the same wavelength calm a child physiologically when they are unsettled. Children are soothed when their fears and anxieties are taken seriously and in their calmness they begin to build resilience to help them deal with future stressful situations. There is some evidence that, if stress hormones like cortisol are activated, and not lowered by warm physical contact or tone of voice at moments of distress, children become unable to regulate their feelings of fear and become overwhelmed or hypervigilant. We have learned that the whole environment needs to be an enabling place where children, parents and other professionals' qualities are respected and valued.

We have learned that children entering group childcare will have established attachment styles and that it can be useful to be able to recognise these and so heighten our awareness to respond sensitively to them. We will notice that children's attachment styles are activated at points of separation and stress but also when attaching to activities, like attempting to join in, explore and play. We know that all children, even when involved in free play, are checking back as they set forth into their world of discovery to see whether adults are supporting their exploration. This may mean they have their back to you and that they are moving away; yet internally they seek the presence of another watching over then and attending to them in their physical absence.

Developing a sense of self

We have learned about the capacity for caring adults to hold a child in mind as being fundamentally important to a child's sense of self. This sense of self is built up during their many journeys to and from their key carer. These are rehearsed many times across a day, a week and in the early months and years of life until a template of security is laid down, through gentle reassuring non-verbal cues from carers who delight in them and enjoy them for who they are rather than just for what they are doing. Every child needs to feel able to step out and explore the world from a sense of certainty that they are the centre of their carer's world.

Meeting the personal, social and emotional needs of parents

Through a culture of respect for parents we are able to contribute in supporting them to provide responsiveness and empathy, overcome their own barriers to education and have meaningful dialogues which establish authentic connections. Parents who struggle to provide their children with appropriate boundaries by working together in partnership with thoughtful and sensitive professionals can be helped with their own containment of loss and separation. It is often easier to support the primary caregiver whose anxiety is visible at the point of separation by making reassuring phone calls home but perhaps the parent who leaves without as much as a backward glance is in need of individualised care too. Working together in partnership with all parents will achieve a positive impact on children's development and learning.

The role of the key person is the foundation stone for all young children who are separated from their primary carer for any length of time. It is the function of the key person to get to know the child intimately and to attend to their primary care – eating, resting and sleeping, being changed and having their toileting needs or nappies attended to. These rituals need to be entered into with a sense of sensitive care and delight in the child for who they are. We need to be aware that we convey much of what we are feeling in our non-verbal body language and so it is important that we express availability at all times. Securely attached children will expect it, anxiously attached children will be checking for it with their built-in radar and not be able to trust in their own capacities without it very close by, and avoidant children will have learned not to expect it. Our knowledge in this area will help us achieve the appropriate response to behaviour that may not appear understandable upon first sight.

Reception class children require this sensitivity too, as they make the transition across different areas of the day and require to feel held and contained in their daily transitions – 'Who is going to be with me now if my teacher has gone to her dinner?'; 'Who are these different grown ups who look after us in the lunch break?'; 'Why haven't we been introduced to them, they feel like strangers to me?'.

When there are moments of unsettledness and children need to seek a haven of security, then adults need to be available to offer comfort, protection and safety. This refuelling goes on from moment to moment and can sometimes be successfully met by a non-verbal signal which confirms to the child you are there for them. It is important that we do not dismiss this need for safety as being 'silly' or 'not being a big girl or boy' as all children's internal needs are unique to them.

The reassurance offered may be offered by physical proximity but it is also communicated through emotional availability by helping a child organise their feelings. This back and forth of the child seeking care and their caregiver as we have mentioned before is rehearsed over and over again through the early years of life until an acceptable space or distance is able to be imagined in the child's mind that can be managed emotionally and is not experienced as a loss or a traumatic absence.

Attending to your own feelings

Practitioners who pay attention to their own feelings (affect responses) whilst caring for children, help themselves to understand why they may sometimes wish to push the more difficult feelings away. For example, if one spends 8 hours in a baby room when the two or three babies in their care are crying and cannot be soothed, then they, like the very young babies in their care, may become overwhelmed. We have understood, therefore, the importance of staff having supervision and collaborative problem-solving and reflective practice groups to help provide a secure base for practitioners so they can refuel emotionally and have a thoughtful space to think through their relationships with children.

Final thoughts

These guiding principles are the foundations upon which learning can flourish. Learning is an integral part of being in relationship with others and the wider environment. We only have to spend a few minutes observing a group of children at play to know that it is serious business. A child's capacity to sustain play and explore involves being supported by caring adults who form the backdrop to their activity. Like the circle of a mother's arms this is the space practitioners create and where all communication takes place. How we communicate all that we observe and experience when guiding and supporting children in their learning is like weaving a rich tapestry, and understanding this and transforming it into a meaningful written account requires great thoughtfulness. It offers an opportunity to engage your imaginations in the same way in which you are nurturing the imaginations of the children in your care. As a practitioner, be brave enough to lead the creative dance in terms of documenting children's learning journeys. Before setting out on any journey we can be certain that there will be one or two interesting diversions and encounters along the way. So record keeping should reflect the tradition of diary or journal writing and become a cherished and joyful account of each child's passion, autonomy, competence, discovery, interaction and interdependence. Meaningful learning journeys are an important communication and have a life beyond the requirements of any curriculum alone and are never abandoned to filing cabinets. They become records of a life lived, read with relish many decades on when they tumble out from amongst our favourite possessions as we are engaged in big life transitions like packing up to move house. These are the books full of our first paint splodges and squiggles which send an electrical current through our very being. These moments allow us to marvel at what we created at such a young age and take us back deep into ourselves to our inherent early creative vitality that has made us into the adult we are becoming.

References and further reading

References

Adamson, P. (2008) The Innocenti Report Card 8: The Childcare Transition, Florence: UNICEF Innocenti Research Centre.

Ainsworth, M.D.S., Blehar, M.C., Waters, E. and Wall, S. (1978) *Patterns of Attachment: A Psychological Study of the Strange Situation*, Hillsdale, NJ; Erlbaum.

Bomber, L.M. (2007) *Inside I'm Hurting*, London: Worth Publishing.

Bowlby, J. (1988) *A Secure Base: Clinical Applications of Attachment Theory*, London: Routledge.

Bowlby, J., Robertson, J. and Rosenbluth, D. (1952) 'A two-year old goes to hospital', *The Psychoanalytic Study of the Child*, 11: 82–94.

Brazelton, T. Berry and Greenspan, S.I. (2000) *The Irreducible Needs of Children*, New York: Da Capo Press.

Brisch K.H. (2002) *Treating Attachment Disorders – From Theory to Therapy*, New York: Guildford Press.

Carr, M. (2001) *Assessment in Early Childhood Settings*, London: Sage.

Cooper, G., Hoffman, K., Marvin, R. and Powell, B. (1998) 'Circle of Security', available online at: circleofsecurity.org

Department for Children, Schools and Families (DCSF) (2007) *Social and Emotional Aspects of Learning (SEAL)*, Nottingham: DCSF Publications.

Department for Children, Schools and Families (DCSF) (2008) *Social and Emotional Aspects of Development. Guidance for Practitioners Working in the Early Years Foundation Stage*, Nottingham: DCSF Publications.

Department for Education and Skills (DfES) (2007a) *Statutory Framework for the Early Years Foundation Stage*, Nottingham: DfES Publications.

Department for Education and Skills (DfES) (2007b) *Practice Guidance for the Early Years Foundation Stage*, Nottingham: DfES Publications.

Department for Education and Skills (DfES) (2007c) *Primary National Strategy – Creating the Picture*, Nottingham: DfES Publications.

Geddes, H. (2006) *Attachment in the Classroom*, London: Worth Publishing.

Goldschmied, E. and Jackson, S. (1994) *People under Three: Young Children in Daycare*, London: Routledge.

Grenier, J., Elfer, P., Manning Morton, J., Dearnley, K. and Wilson, D. (2008) 'The key person in reception classes and small nursery settings', Appendix 1, *Social and Emotional Aspects of Development – Guidance for Practitioners Working in the Foundation Stage*, Nottingham: DCSF Publications.

Hanko, G. (1999) *Increasing Competence through Collaborative Problem Solving*, London: David Fulton.

Hawkins, P. and Shohet R. (2006) *Supervision in the Helping Professions*, Maidenhead: Open University Press.

Holmes, J. (1993) *John Bowlby and Attachment Theory*, London: Brunner-Routledge.

Hughes, A. (2006) *Developing Play for the Under 3s*, London: David Fulton.

Jackson, S. (2009) 'Close to you', *Nursery World*, April 30.

McCluskey, U. (2005) *To be Met as a Person: The Dynamics of Attachment in Professional Encounters*, London: Karnac.

Robertson, J. and Robertson, J. (1968) *Young Children in Brief Separation – John,* distributed by Concord Video and film Council Ltd.

Rutter, M. (1981) *Maternal Deprivation Reassessed*, Harmondsworth: Penguin Books.

Stern, D.N. (1985) *The Interpersonal World of the Infant*, New York: Basic Books.

Trevarthen, C. (1974) 'Conversations with a two-month-old', *New Scientist*, 62: 230–35.

Tronick, E.Z. (1989) 'Emotions and emotional communication in infants', *American Psychologist*, 44: 112–19.

Winnicott, D.W. (1958) *Collected Papers – Through Paediatrics to Psycho-Analysis*, London: Tavistock.

Winnicott, D.W. (1965) *The Maturation Process and the Facilitating Environment*, London: Karnac.

Further reading

Gerhardt, S. (2004) *Why Love Matters: How Affection Shapes a Baby's Brain*, Hove, Sussex: Brunner-Routledge.

Greenhaugh, P. (1994) *Emotional Growth and Learning*, New York: Routledge.

Grenier, J. (1999) '(Extract from) All about … developing positive relations with children', *Nursery World*, Sept., pp. 12–13.

Sunderland, M. (2006) *The Science of Parenting*, London: Dorling Kindersley.

Further DVD resource material

Life at Two – Attachments, key people and development, Siren Films Ltd, 2009.

Secure Attachment and the Key Person in Daycare: A basic guide to attachment theory by Richard Bowlby. Copyright and reproduction rights R. Bowlby 2009.

Index